LINUX
Command-Line
for Beginners

A Comprehensive Step-by-Step
Starting Guide to Learn Linux
from Scratch to Bash Scripting
and Shell Programming

By Dylan Mach

Table of Contents

Introduction

Congratulations on purchasing your copy of *LINUX Command-Line for Beginners: A Comprehensive Step-By-Step Starting Guide to Learn Linux from Scratch to Bash Scripting and Shell Programming* and thank you for doing so.

Linux is in virtually everything we use today. If you are a beginner or you are just starting to learn everything about Linux operating system, you will soon realize that downloading this eBook is a smart way into having a clear understanding of the world of Linux as well as several of its distributions. Usually, navigating through the Linux command-line can be quite tricky. In this book, you will see multiple approaches that you can model to have a smooth operation with Linux. Also, certain Linux distributions you can use not only as a beginner but also those that can function if you attempt to use it on your old system. Ultimately, this book takes a step further to analyze basic Linux shell commands as well as shell scripting.

To this end, some of the chapters in this book will discuss Linux user management and administration, where it examines some of the duties of Linux system administrator, including handling directories, users extensively, and files, basic bash commands, root, or superuser management, and so much more. Also, this book will discuss Linux file functions as well as defining the three types of Linux file ownership, permissions, and SSH commands. You will learn about other SSH commands, Linux terminals, editors, and shell.

With a clear perception of directories, file managers, and editors out of the way, this book will discuss how you can create a file for tar gzip from the command-line, how you can mount and unmounts media, and also Linux data manipulation.

On the shelves, there are several books on Linux Command-line, and for making this book your choice, we will like to appreciate the gesture. From our end, we are striving to see that this book provides you with all the practical and necessary information you will need to succeed. Once again, thank you!

Chapter 1: What is Linux and Why Using It?

Strengthening almost everything from mobile phones, servers, and PCs, Linux is a standard operating system that people commonly use. Indeed, all over the world, several individuals use Linux in all fields and applications you can imagine. Linux has been around since the 90s. From your TV stick to the fridge and everything, Linux runs everything. And much of the internet has support from Linux. Since the computer operating system has powered several innovations, many scientific breakthroughs have Linux to thank. Even though for decades, Linux has been supplying secure, reliable OS duties, the word "Linux" has no familiarity with the general public.

But Linux operating system is everywhere, from enterprise servers to home desktops, home appliances, supercomputers, cars, and smartphones. Everywhere, you will find Linux, and it is on your television, Roku devices, refrigerators, and thermostats. For being one of the stress-free, most secure and reliable operating system available, Linux prides itself as a preferred platform running embedded systems, servers, and desktops all over the world.

What is Linux OS?

In the first place, what do you understand by an OS or operating system? In a physical computer, the management of the hardware is the duty of the computer code known as the operating system. Between the hardware and software, the operating system exists as a layer. Also, in assembler, communicating with a graphics card or addressing a CPU is not what most people want to know. And what acts as a middleman is an operating system like Windows or Linux.

Therefore, Linux, like Mac OS, iOs, and Windows, is an operating system. Essentially, Linux operating system powers Android, which is the most popular platform in the world. The software is likely not to function without the operating system since, as an operating system, Linux manages the communication between the hardware and software.

There are so many different pieces that Linux operating system comprises and they are:

- **Applications** – not all the complete array of apps that the desktop environments provide. As such, you can quickly find and install several thousands of software that are high-quality through Linux, typical of macOS and Windows. There are simplicity and centralization in the application installation by most modern Linux distributions. For example, typical of GNOME Software, there is Ubuntu Software Center by Ubuntu Linux that, from one centralized platform, speeds up the discovery and installation of apps among thousands of them for users.

- **Desktop environment** – users can interact with this piece. You can choose from several desktop environments like Xfce, KDE, Enlightenment, Pantheon, Mate, Cinnamon, GNOME, and so on. There are built-in applications for each desktop environment, including games, web browsers, configuration tools, and file managers.

- **Graphical server** – on your monitor, you will get a graphic display with this subsystem. It is known as X or X-server by many people.

- **Daemons** – after logging into the desktop or startup during boot, these are background services such as scheduling, sound, printing, and so on.

- **Init system** – user space is bootstrapped by this subsystem, and the control of daemons is in its charge.

As such, systemd, as the most controversial, is an init system most widely used. When the bootloader, like Unified Bootloader or GRUB, handles the initial booting, the init system manages the boot process.

- **OS Kernel** – kernel can be referred to as a complete piece known as Linux for the management of the peripheral devices, memory, CPU, and the core of the system is the kernel.

- **Bootloader** – this software manages the process of the computer boot. It is a splash screen that pops up in the operating system and soon goes away to boot for most users.

- **OS Shell** – the shell is what we use to tell our operating system the things we want it to do. As the command line by many, you use text to instruct the OS. However, the code of command-lines is known by quite a few people. As such, this caused people to stay away from using Linux. The modern distribution of Linux changed this since, just like Windows, Linux will use a desktop.

Why Using Linux?

Most people ask this question almost all the time. When the OS that ships virtually all servers, laptops, and desktops function correctly, why would anyone bother to learn a wholly different computing environment? The answer to that question will pose another question rather than a response; are you okay with the working of your current operating system? Or are you struggling with license fees, costly repairs, crashes, slowdowns, malware, and viruses? For you, Linux may be the perfect platform if you find yourself struggling with the above. On the planet, right now, the most reliable computer ecosystem is Linux. For a desktop platform, you will have a perfect solution when you combine such the entry's zero cost with reliability. As there isn't any payment for server licensing or the software, you can have as many computers as you like to install Linux. Also, you won't have any requirement to make any payment to access Linux.

Besides that, what about having as long as you want, a stress-free, stable operating system if you are not bothered about the zero cost implications? There hasn't been an issue of viruses, malware, or ransomware by so many people using Linux, both on server platform and desktop, for more than two decades. The thing is, such attacks have no power over Linux. If only the kernel is updated, they are necessary for server reboots. And it may not be entirely out of the ordinary for a Linux server to go for years without being rebooted. You will surely enjoy dependability and stability when recommended updates are strictly followed.

Also, our computers have most of the desktop operating systems we use, and changing the operating system is something we rarely probe. What's more? Learning a new operating system is not what most people are inclined to do. However, here are some of the reasons you need to try out Linux:

A host of different distributions

There is variance in the Linux different distributions or editions. Some are for server software, while others are designed for desktop use. And while some are designed with beginners in mind, others have their focus on the advanced users. Most Linux editions otherwise referred to as distributions, use USB drive for installation, an optical disk, or can be downloaded for free. The Linux distributions are quite endless. Though some popular choices are openSUSE and Debian, the default preferences for desktop users are mostly Linux Mint, Arch, and Fedora. Courtesy of Ubuntu Unity, Ubuntu becomes one of the most modern Linux distributions. Through the inclusion of openSUSE, you can get a more traditional Linux look with KDE. Also, it is quite a long list if you are looking for the list of server Linux OS. CentOS, SUSE Enterprise, Ubuntu Server, and Red Hat are some of the most well-known distributions. However, you may need to invest in some money with the use of some Linux server distributions as licensing may be required to use Red Hat. But, quite essential for your business is the support, which you get for your license fee in return.

Linux is the same as freedom

There is a need to have the definition of an open source as equivalent to Linux. There are a set of principles that any software follows, such as:

- For any of your modified software, copies will have no restrictions

- The software distribution will have no limit

- There will be permission to make any changes needed by you, examine it, as well as study and disassemble the software

- Irrespective of your goals or motive for running it, the full freedom to run the software

Primarily, open-source software does not correlate to a community, and you need to understand that. Linux is built by this community, and Linux enjoys robust maintenance from that community. As such, people made Linux as software for the rest of the world, if you are wondering what Linux is and what has brought about the popularity of Linux. It is all about this philosophy of open source.

Linux is excellent in reliability

Since it is quite reliable, for system administrators, life is comfortable with the use of Linux. As such, not every day that you will need to monitor your server, and there are no worries with running it. Also, without impacting the whole Linux OS, you can often restart the separate services because of the way they built Linux. You must rely on a tool called an operating system, going by convention. You can have the game-changing effect of reliability that Linux brings with it if the cost isn't the most significant factor for you. And what is the biggest benefit of the Linux operating system? The biggest reason to adopt Linux is that Linux has overall immunity to random issues of an operating system as well as malicious software and viruses and also its inherent reliability.

Linux saves you money

For you to try out Linux, you won't have to pay anything since Linux has a collaborative and open-source nature. Without licensing payment, it doesn't matter if you have multiple computers; you can go ahead and have the operating system installed freely on them. For many Linux distributions, whether desktop or server editions, this is simply the situation. For example, just for the software installation on one server, concerning the version of 2012, you will have to part with $1,200 to use the Windows Server of Microsoft. You will have additional client access license charges if you are the type that wants several clients to have access to it. And what about the required licenses for you to run web, Windows-based services, etc.? Contrary to that, there is an inclusion of open-source server software in Linux distributions that comes without any cost. Also, without any payment for licensing, you can make use of several web pages. And with just a few clicks, you can have up and running, an entirely efficient Linux web server.

You can easily try Linux

Linux is quite simple to try when you are prepared to experiment with it. If you are feeling hesitant, there's no need for you to have your Windows discarded. You may want to give the preferred operating system a whirl with a live DVD or drive before installing on the hard drive of your PC on a Linux distribution. You will have to install a flash drive or DVD on a Linux distribution, a bootable system. Then, instead of your drive, have your system configured to boot from that. The fuss and muss are quite minimal as you quickly test-drive some operating systems of Linux, and the primary storage drive you have is safe since it doesn't touch it.

Linux can run on outdated systems

A while ago, they have Windows XP tossed to the wolves, and the Windows Vista is swiftly on the brink to the end. However, some outdated PCs and many people rely on them. If you select a lightweight distribution designed for aging PCs, it can breathe a new life into your computer as well as splashes updated OS on your system. For old PCs, you can choose Lubuntu or Puppy Linux. You will also notice that there is nothing stressful concerning the transition. Since they designed it for Windows XP refugees, there is abundance when it comes to accessing Linux alternatives. For the mimic of feel and look of the operating system of Microsoft, which is highly revered, these distributions provide dedicated "Windows XP Modes."

More sophisticated than before

The desktop's fundamental values are what most main Linux distributors follow. So, the established interface of the PC gets the spit-polish from distributions such as Linux Mint and Fedora, while with the Windows 8 disaster, Microsoft enraged the world. People can wrap their head around some Linux distributions if Windows 7 and Windows XP is their preference. It is typical for them to switch to Linux because of the learning curve that they will need to use Windows 8 or Windows 10. There is also a similarity with the Start menu of the long-established Windows with the Start menu of Linux Mint. Most fundamentally, using it with PC hardware, there is an eradication of the widespread incompatibility of Linux, particularly audio components and networking. Even though with Intel's Secure Boot enabled to have additional steps performed for the installation of Linux on your system, there is a wide range of PC hardware and modern PCs that work with most Linux operating systems. Better yet, to know whether it will work or not before you go ahead with any installation, you can have Linux distributions tested on your system to remember your preference.

There are several compelling reasons you might want to consider to try out Linux on your computer, or at least, give it a hassle-free trial run. And if you are set to go ahead with it, let's discuss the Linux distributions and how you can push forward and make the proper installation of Linux in the next chapter.

Chapter 2: Linux Distributions and Types of Installations

You may have no clear answer if you are asking for the best Linux distributions since, in one way or the other, there are several numbers of Linux distributions, and coming up with an exact amount also can be quite tricky. As some of them appear to be unique, others are simply a clone of one another. Well, that is the beauty of Linux, even if it's a mess. However, you don't have to worry because, below, you will find the list of the best Linux distributions even when there are thousands of them around. Since there is always something for everyone, we must categorize these distributions.

Linux distribution for multi-purpose

For both servers and desktops, as an advanced/beginner-friendly OS, you can utilize some Linux distributions. Thus, you will read below about a separate segment of these distributions, and they are:

Debian:

As an excellent distribution itself, Debian has its base on Ubuntu. Debian tends to be working correctly for not only the desktop but also the servers. Though by scanning through the official documentation, you can quickly get started, it may not be the ideal operating system for beginners. There are some necessary enhancements and several changes introduced by the recent release of Debian 10 Buster. So, test-drive it for you to see!

Manjaro:

The Arch Linux provides the source for Manjaro. For newbies, Manjaro makes it quite easy to use Arch Linux even though it is tailored for advanced users. So have no worries. This Linux distribution is indeed beginner-friendly and straightforward. There are a bunch of useful built-in GUI applications, as well as a fantastic user interface. While downloading Manjaro, there's an option of selecting a desktop environment. For Manjaro, most people have a preference for the KDE desktop.

Fedora:

The two editions that Fedora provides are separate. It offers for servers and also for laptops/desktops. Those are Fedora Server and Fedora Workstation. Well, Fedora may be your option if you wish to opt for a user-friendly with a possibility of a learning curve for a snappy desktop OS. Anyways, your server can get a fresh breath of a new life when you choose Fedora if you are looking for an operating system for Linux.

Advanced users best Linux distributions

First, before you begin your exploration into Linux distributions that are designed for advanced users only, you need to get comfortable troubleshooting your way to resolve issues with the different package commands and managers. Indeed, there will be a need for you to collect specific requirements if you are a professional. However, it will worth your while to check out these distributions if, as a standard user, you have been using Linux for some time.

Slackware:

Though still delighting in the preference of many people, one of the oldest Linux distributions is Slackware. You may want to consider using Slackware for setting up an ideal environment for yourself if you intend to develop or compile software. Slackware tends to be a fantastic choice for advanced users, even with a significant decrease in the number of developers and users utilizing it. Also, it is believed that Slackware will continue to carry its flagship as one of the best Linux distributions out there with the current news of it getting a Patreon page.

Gentoo:

Gentoo Linux is quite compulsory for anyone who knows how to compile the source code. Though there is a required necessary technical knowledge to make it work, Gentoo is a lightweight distribution. If you need to know some information about it, you can obtain it through the official handbook. However, to make the most of it might take you a lot of time to figure if you are not sure of what you are doing.

Arch Linux:

This distribution comes with a huge learning curve even though it is a powerful yet simple distribution. Everything you need may not be installed at a time, much unlike others. You will have to add packages required as you configure the system. Also, without GUI, there are a set of commands you will need to follow when you are installing Arch Linux. Also, it may be quite essential to have a clear understanding of some critical things to do after you install Arch Linux if you wish to go ahead with the installation. It's indeed useful to say that there is an active community behind Arch Linux in addition to all the simplicity and versatility. As such, you won't have any need to worry if you run into a problem.

Older computers' best Linux distributions

You can make use of some of the best Linux distributions available if you don't wish to upgrade your system or have an old one lying around. Here are some of the best distributions you can use for your old computers.

Sparky Linux:

For low-end systems, based on Debian, Sparky Linux tends to be a perfect Linux distribution. Different users can enjoy several special editions or varieties provided by Sparky Linux, as well as a fast streaming experience. For example, it rolls releases specific to a group of users while offering a stable version with varieties. For gamers, one familiar type for them is the Sparky Linux GameOver since a bunch of pre-installed games is included in it.

antiX:

As a lightweight Linux distribution and partially responsible for MX Linux, both new and old computers can use antiX.

Though working quite correctly, the UI of antiX is not that impressive. Without the need to install it, antiX can be utilized as live CD distribution, and it is based on Debian. For you not to lose settings with every reboot, you can save the settings as opposed to some other distributions. Not only that, using its feature of "Live persistence," your root directory can also have some changes saved by you. As such, antiX can be your choice if you intend to offer a snappy user experience on old hardware with the use of a live-USB distribution.

Bodhi:

Though it runs well on older configurations, unlike Ubuntu, it is well on top of Ubuntu that they designed and built Bodhi Linux. As a continuation of the Enlightenment 17 desktop, Bodhi Linux's Moksha Desktop is its main highlight. The fast and intuitive streaming is the typical experience users will get for using it. On your older systems, you can as well give it a try even though people's opinion of it is not for personal use.

Solus Budgie:

It is an impressive lightweight desktop OS with Solus 4 Fortitude as a recent major release. Desktop environments such as MATE or GNOME are natural for this when you want to opt into them. However, while being light on system resources, as a beginners' full-fledged Linux distribution, Solus Budgie happens to be one of the favorites of so many people.

Puppy Linux:

One of the smallest distributions you can see out there is Puppy Linux. If you want your outdated system to have a quick system execution, you can give it a try. With the addition of several new useful features, the user experience has improved over the years.

As for some of the lightweight Linux distributions, other options you can try out in this category are Peppermint, Lubuntu, and Linux Lite.

Best distributions of Linux server

Enterprise support, performance, and stability are all that are essential when it comes to a Linux distributions' choice for servers. However, you need to pay attention to some of these recommendations, whether the purpose is for something crucial or a web server when installing it.

CentOS:

For RHEL, you will need to subscribe. Nevertheless, since the sources of Red Hat Linux have been derived from it, RHEL's community edition is quite similar to CentOS. Also, it is a free and open-source as well. For sometimes now, it tends to be an excellent preference. It is considerably less parallel to the number of hosting providers using it. However, people's opinion of CentOS is that of a reliable Linux distribution since its software packages are the latest. On several cloud platforms, CentOS images can be found. You can as well decide on the CentOS image that is self-hosted, which it offers if you don't.

SUSE Linux enterprise server:

There's a need to separate this distribution from OpenSuSE, and as such, there's no need to worry. Maintained by the community, OpenSUSE is an open-source distribution even when everything comes under a standard brand "SUSE." For cloud-based servers, one of the most popular solutions is the SUSE Linux enterprise server. And to manage your open-source solution and to get priority support, you may need to go for a subscription.

Linux Red Hat:

For organizations and businesses, the top-notch platform is the Linux Red Hat. For servers, the highly prevalent range may not be Red hat if we go by the numbers. However, Lenovo, for instance, is among those that have their reliance on RHEL as the primary selection of enterprise users. Technically, there is a correlation between Red Hat and Fedora. And for RHEL to have it on it, anything that Red Hats supports gets tested on Fedora. For you to be sure it will suit your needs, the official documentation of the distribution is worth checking.

Ubuntu servers:

Your server can get unique options depending on where you want it. Ubuntu Cloud may be the perfect ideal for an optimized solution to run Google Cloud Platform, Azure, AWS, and some others. In either case, you can have it installed on your server if you want to opt for Ubuntu Server packages. However, judging by the number, when it comes to deployment on the cloud, the highly popular Linux distribution is Ubuntu. And unless you have particular requirements, the recommendation will be the LTS editions.

As options for a few of the distributions mentioned above, Debian and Fedora are some of the distributions to explore.

Beginners' best Linux distributions

This segment deals with a list of distributions that are quite easy to use. Without the requirement of knowing any tips or commands, you can begin using it right away, and there's no need to dig deeper.

Pop!_OS:

Computer science professionals or developers will experience an excellent pick by Sytem76 from Pop!_OS. If you are beginning to use Linux, it is also quite a great choice as it is not limited to coders. Though the UI feels smooth and a lot more intuitive, it is based on Ubuntu. Also, it enforces full-disk encryption out of the box in addition to the UI.

Zorin OS:

One of the most intuitive and good-looking OS for desktop is another Ubuntu-based distribution, which is Zorin OS. Notably, the recommendation for users without any Linux background will be this distribution after Zorin OS 15 release. It also comes baked in as well as a lot of GUI-based applications. Though ensure to choose the "Lite" edition because you can also install it on older PCs. There are also "Ultimate," "Education," and "Core" editions. However, consider getting the Ultimate version if you intend to help improve Zorin and also support the developers. Otherwise, select the Core edition for free.

MX Linux:

It has been a while now that MX Linux has been in the game. On Distrowatch.com, at present, MX Linux is a highly preferred Linux distribution. You will be amazed as to how you will get familiar with it if you haven't used it before. With Xfce being its desktop environment and also based on Debian, an increasingly popular Linux distribution is MX Linux, unlike Ubuntu. Also, any Mac/Windows user can easily use it as it is packed with several GUI tools in addition to its excellent stability. Also, for installation with one-click facilitation, the package manager is ideally tailored for this. And as one of the sources that are already in the package manager, you will see Flathub there, and in no time, you can install it after searching for Flatpak packages.

elementary OS:

An elegant Linux distribution out there is the elementary OS. It is easy to get comfortable with it if you have already used a Mac-powered system because the UI has a similar resemblance to MacOS. While keeping the performance in mind and also looking as pretty as possible, delivering a user-friendly Linux environment is the focus of this distribution that is based on Ubuntu.

Linux Mint:

Among beginners, another popular Linux is Linux Mint Cinnamon. When Windows XP was discontinued, as a result, many users opted for it since there's a resemblance between Windows XP and the default Cinnamon desktop. It has the applications available for Ubuntu since it is on Ubuntu that

Linux Mint is grounded. It becomes a prominent choice for new users of Linux because of the ease of use and simplicity.

Ubuntu:

One of the most undoubtedly popular Linux distributions is Ubuntu, and on several laptops available, you can even find it pre-installed. You will get comfortable with its user interface. As per your requirements, you can easily customize the look of it if you play around. Mainly, theme installation is also another option for you. When you want to get started with Ubuntu, you will need to learn more about it. Also, Ubuntu users have a massive community that you can find in addition to what it provides. So, go to a subreddit or the forum if you face any issue. You need to check out some coverage online on Ubuntu in case they require direct solutions in no time.

Ultimately, you can give some of these distributions recommended above a try. And quite honestly, the choices will be subjective depending on personal preferences to each of them even when there are quite several Linux distributions that deserve mention.

Server Roles and Types of Installations

Since more operating systems have a great connection with it, this attribute is a unique feature of Linux. Thus, you can have other OS running alongside Linux. With more operating systems in place and for the installation of Linux, the general process of installation is to install Linux again. When you do that, the computer will have 100 percent resources dedication to run Linux. However, as part of an OS sequence which is obtainable on a computer, it is not quite hard to have Linux installed. Also, as an approach you can use to run or install on a computer any distribution of Linux, you can make use of some of these approaches below;

Linux fresh installation

One popular method of installation available is this method. From a DVD/CD, you will install Linux after formatting the hard drive of your computer when you jump into this technique. Then, it is only on the operating system of your computer that Linux will then run. Available methods of installation are:

- PXE

- Kickstart

- Network installation through HTTP, FTP, or NFS

- Hard drive

- CD-ROM

Linux as a VM inside another operating system

Inside another operating system, you may want to consider running Linux as a VM if you prefer to run your favorite open-source software or want an easy way to access a Linux desktop even when you like your current, non-Linux desktop OS. You will need to download and install a Virtual Server application as a simple step, although there are several ways to go by it. Then, under the host software, install your Linux distribution. Thus, you may perform on Linux everything you can do with your other operating system. Even when your other operating systems don't offer some things, there are a lot of things that Linux can provide you.

Live DVD/CD booting Linux

You may choose to try Linux from a Live DVD/CD when you want to retain your primary operating system and to see if you like it, you want to give Linux a try. As a Live CD, several Linux installations offer this running or downloading. As such, from the DVD/CD, Linux will run as an entire operating system that is quite bootable. And instead of running it on a hard drive, you can load your files into the memory of your computer. That means, from a DVD/CD, Linux can be run and then exclusive of any variance, return to its old OS of your system as you remove the DVD/CD when you reboot your computer.

Until you discover your preferred choice, you can easily sample some Linux distributions.

Dual-booting

You will have a dual booting system when you want to install Linux and also keep an existing operating system as well. You will then need to decide which one you would like to boot into during the boot process since you will have a PC that can use two different operating systems.

By now, you must be having a bit of understanding of Linux, as well as some distributions that you can use them. Now, it is time to take things further and introduce to you Linux Kernel as well as the operating systems.

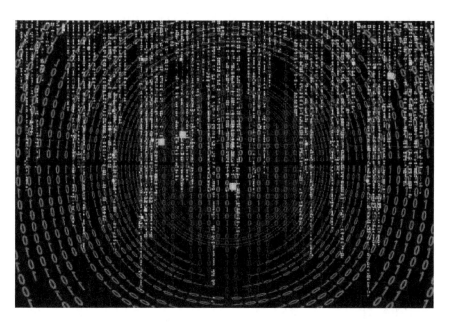

Chapter 3: Introduction to Linux Kernel and Operating System

By what means does a computer manage the most complex tasks with such accuracy and efficiency? Well, the short and simple answer is that a computer does everything with the help of the operating system. The operating system makes life easier and performs different tasks through the efficient use of hardware resources. At a high level, there are two parts we can divide the OS. The first part will be the utility programs, while the other is the kernel. The kernel services some of the system resources requests like network connectivity, memory, storage, CPU, and so on, as asked by the various user space processes. And in Linux/GNU, there will be an exploration of the loadable kernel modules by this column. Since the whole operating system solely run in supervisor mode, this makes Linux kernel monolithic. With each subsystem responsible for performing specific tasks, it consists of several subsystems, even though the kernel is a single process. Broadly, these following tasks are performed by any kernel.

Dynamically loadable kernel modules

To ensure that our system is up-to-date, most times, we install security patches and kernel updates. A reboot is often necessary in the case of MS Windows. However, this is far from being suitable. For example, when it is in a production server, the machine cannot be rebooted. Then, without a system reboot, wouldn't it be ideal for removing or adding functionality from or to the kernel on-the-fly? For the kernel modules, the Linux kernels work on the dynamic unloading and loading. And at runtime, any code piece is a kernel module that you can add to the kernel. Without any interruption, when the system is up and running, you can unload and load the modules. You can use the `insmod` command to dynamically link a kernel module to the running kernel and also unlink it by using the `rmmod` command, as an object code.

Networking

One of the vital parts of the operating system is the networking because it works with data transfer between hosts and also allows communication. As routing functionality gets enabled by it, it is also through it that network packets get transmitted, identified, and collected.

Device control

There are several devices required for any computer system. However, for the layer to offer functionality, there is a need for a device driver to make the devices usable. Video/audio drivers, Bluetooth drivers, graphics drivers, and so on are some of the types of drivers present.

File system

The file system heavily influences the Linux/GNU system. Nearly everything is a file in Linux/GNU. Also, conventional for the organization of data hierarchically, journaling and compression of data, deletion, and creation of files, and so on are the storage relation requirements controlled by this subsystem. All primary file systems have the support of the Linux kernel, such as MS Windows NTFS.

Memory management

This subsystem handles every related request. The pages are chunks of fixed size as divided from available memory, and on any demand, can be de-allocated or allocated from or to the process. As it creates the illusions of contiguous ample address space to a physical address space, it also maps the process virtual address with the help of the memory management unit, MMU.

Process management

The life-cycle gets this subsystem to handle the process. Through inter-process communication, it allows data sharing and connection between processes as it also destroys and creates processes. Also, it enables resource sharing and schedules processes with the help of the process scheduler.

Some Useful Utilities

For the provision of useful information about the kernel modules, Linux/GNU offers several user-space utilities. Now, let's dive into them.

dmesg: though it is a different methodology that the kernel uses, it is on the standard output stream that any user-space program displays its output, i.e., */dev/stdout*. For us to manage the contents of the ring buffer, with the use of the dmesg command, the kernel appends its output to the ring buffer.

modinfo: as a command-line argument, the module that passes such process displays the information by this command. For modules, it searches the */lib/modules/<version>* directory if the argument is not on a filename. Also, it is on the field:value format that modinfo shows each attribute of the module.

It is essential to note that the kernel version is *<version>*, and it is through the execution of the *uname -r* command that we can obtain it.

rmmod: when you want to unload modules from the kernel, you can make use of this command. It is only when the current module is not in use that you can unload. Also used to unload modules forcibly, the *-force* or *-f* has the support of *rmmod*. However, the danger in using this option is extreme, and to remove modules, you can still make use of a safer way. As it waits until the module is no longer used, *rmmod* will isolate the module with the option of *--wait* or *-w*.

The System Preparation

Now, it's action time. An environment for development is all we need to create now. We will have a Debian-based Linux/GNU distribution like Ubuntu and CentOS of a PRM-based Linux/GNU distribution installed as the required packages.

CentOS installation

As a root user and by implementing the command below, the first step is to have the compiler for *GCC* installed:

```
[root]# yum -y install GCC
```

Now, the packages to develop the kernel are the next in the installation level:

```
[root]# yum -y install kernel-devel
```

In conclusion, the utility of the make comes next for the installation:

```
[root]# yum -y install make
```

Ubuntu installation

The compiler for *GCC* is the first in the installation line:

```
[mickey] Sudo apt-get install GCC
```

Then, the packages for kernel development come next:

```
[mickey] Sudo apt-get install kernel-package
```

Then, the utility of the make installation:

```
[mickey] Sudo apt-get install make
```

And we have the kernel module

Now, we have prepared our system. Then, we will need to have the initial module of a kernel written. Using the following contents, use *hello.c* to have the file saved when you open your favorite text editor:

```
#include <linux/kernel.h>

#include <linux/module.h>
```

```
Int init_module (void)

{

printk(KERN_INFO □Hello, World !!!\n□);

return 0;
}

void cleanup_module(void)

{

printk(KERN_INFO □Exiting …\n□);

}

MODULE_LICENSE(□GPL□);

MODULE_AUTHOR(□Narendra Kangralkar.□);

MODULE_DESCRIPTION(□Hello world module.□);
```

At least, there are two functions for any module. The function of cleanup is the first and second initialization. As such, a cleanup utility is `cleanup_module()` while the initialization function is `init_module()`. And once you load the module and before the module is unloaded, there will be a call for the initialization function, and then the call for the function of cleanup. Other macros, as well as *MODULE_LICENSE*, are quite easy to follow. Relatively the same as `printf()`, the user-space is the syntax, which is a `printk()`. However, at a regular productivity stream, it doesn't print messages, unlike `printf()`. Instead, it is the kernel's ring buffer that receives messages that it appends. There is a priority from each declaration of `printk()`. In the example, KERN_INFO priority is used. And between the string of format and KERN_INFO, you won't see any comma (,) there. Without the presence of unconditional priority, you can make use of *DEFAULT_MESSAGE_LOGLEVEL* priority. As an indication of success, there is the return 0 in `init_module()` final declaration.

cleanup_module() and *init_modules()* are the name of the cleanup and initialization functions. However, we can make use of whichever name in place of cleanup and initialization function with *(>= 2.3.13)*, which is the new kernel. For rearward similarity, there is support for these dated names. In place of the register of the cleanup and initialization functions, the macros provided by the kernel are *module_exit* and *module_init*. Now, with the names of the preference we have for cleanup and initialization functions, let's rewrite the same module:

```
#include <linux/kernel.h>
#include <linux/module.h>

Static int_init hello_init(void)

{

printk(KERN_INFO □Hello, World !!!\n□);

return 0;

}

static void_exit hello_exit(void)

{

printk(KERN_INFO □Exiting …\n□);

return 0;

}

static void_exit hello_exit(void)

{

printk(KERN_INFO □Exiting …\n□);

}

module_init(hello init);

module_exit(hello_exit);

MODULE_LICENSE(□GPL□);
```

28

```
MODULE_AUTHOR(□Narendra Kangralkar.□);

MODULE_DESCRIPTION(□Hello world module.□);

MODULE_VERSION(□1.0□);
```

What we have in this place is that the cleanup and initialization functions imply the `_exit` and `_init` keywords.

Module loading and compilation

Right now, the procedure for module compilation needs to be understood. We will make use of the build system of the kernel for the compilation of the kernel module. Before you have it saved as `Makefile`, you may want to have the process of the collection written down as you, once again, open your favorite text editor. Here, you need to pay attention because you must have a similar directory for the modules of kernel `Makefile` and `hello.c`.

There is a requirement for the kernel headers for us to have the modules built. From the kernel's source, the kernel build system is incited by the above `makefile`, and finally, to complete the module, the `makefile` of the kernel may have our `Makefile` invoked. You can complete the process as name `hello.ko` for the kernel module you develop since, to have the module built, all the requirements are now in our possession.

The first compilation of the first module of the kernel is now successful. Now, it is time to examine the way to, inside a kernel, unload and also load this module. You must take note that to unload or load kernel modules; we need to acquire the root user privileges. You will need to have the command `insmod` executed when you change to the mode of a super-user to load a module as you will see the following:

```
[root]# insmod hello.ko
```

And the success job has been done by `insmod`. However, the output is necessary for us to find. It is the ring buffer of the kernel that the output is appended. Well, through the execution of `dmesg` command, we can as well find out:

```
[root]# dmesg
Hello, World !!!
```

Also, we can verify if or not the module is stocked by using the command `lsmod`:

```
[root]# lsmod | grep hello
hello 859 0
```

All that is required of you is to check the output of the `dmesg` command as you have the command `rmmod` executed. As you see below, to unload the module from the kernel. Now, through the function of cleanup, you will see the message from `dmesg`. Some macros within the module give us the module's information. And in such an attractively configured style below, displaying the information is the command `modinfo`.

How to identify the process' PID

For us to identify a Process ID, which is the existing process's PID, we may need to compose one more module of the kernel. In the header, defined as the `<linux/sched.h>`, it is in the structure of the `task_struct` that the related information of the kernel stocks all progression. As an indicator of the existing process, it offers an *existing* variable. You are only required to have the `current->pid` variable value printed to have the current process PID identified. The `(pid.c)`, a complete code of working, will then be given.

In the object file's name, with a slight modification, similar to an original `makefile` is the `Makefile`. With the use of the `dmesg` command, have the output squared after inserting the module and then make the compilation.

Bridging several files with a module

From a single file, the module compilation has been explored. However, dividing the module into multiple files can be quite convenient, and for a single module, we have multiple source files in a large project. For the building of a module that extends over two files, we must understand the process. From the file `hello.c`, we can divide the cleanup and initialization functions to become two individual files such as `cleanup.c` and `startup.c`. The change will be like this for `cleanup.c`. Then, we will have the exciting part concerning the two modules, the `Makefile`. Self-explanatory enough is the `Makefile`. Now, in our proposition: with the use of `cleanup.o` and `startup.o`, develop the final kernel object. It is time for the compilation and testing of the module. When we utilize the command `modinfo`, we may display module information. From each module, author-related information, license, description, and versions are now shown through the command `modinfo`. It is now the time for output verification by unloading and loading the module for `final.ko`.

The best place to learn more about modules is the kernel source code. When you go online, you can download the latest source code. Right now, we will have to go ahead and discuss in detail how you can install Linux on Virtual Machines. Let's go!

Chapter 4: Installing Linux on Virtual Machine

You might not be sure about dual booting even after installing Linux when you try it from a live CD/DVD. It can be quite useful to use a virtual machine, VM, to install your preferred Linux operating system. What this translates into is that the conditions of a hardware environment are the replication of a software environment. With the limit only coming from the components inside it, the base of your physical PC's hardware is the environment. For example, with two cores, it may be impossible to have on a processor, a virtual four-core CPU. However, on a CPU equipped computer, the outcomes can be far superior, while virtualization can be achieved on many systems. As there are several of them in Windows, for the installation of the Linux operating system to be easy, several virtualization tools are quite available. The one among them to produces the significantly accomplished virtual machine applications is VMware. Now, with the use of VMware Workstation Player, it is time to discover the process of Linux installation in Windows.

VMware Workstation Player Installation

In the initial phase, you will need to have the latest version of the VMware Workstation Player tool downloaded by going to the VMware website. With the 64-bit version, it is about 80 MB for the release of 12.5. For home, personal, and non-commercial use as an evaluation version, you can find VMware Workstation Player for free. For non-profit organizations and students, getting value from the free version is all that makes VMware delighted. As for the functionality factor, the standard virtual machine tasks hosts everything included in the VMware Workstation Player. However, for the business of all levels are the extensive selections of virtualization solutions offered by VMware.

Then, it's time for installation after you must have downloaded VMware Workstation Player. An Enhanced

Keyboard Driver installation option will be available for you as you get your guide from a standard installation wizard. Also, you will be able to handle the international keyboards provided by this feature. Just in case, you will see that it's worth installing even as you mightn't need it in the first place. When prompted, restart Windows as you proceed via the installation wizard.

Desired Linux operating system selection

For the kind of Linux that you want to give a try, you likely know it. In a VM, while you will find some Linux distributions not especially suitable, others will be. Conventionally, in VMware, for ARM architecture like the Raspberry Pi, running Linux distributions may not be possible. As such, with the x64 and x86, you may not be able to virtualize the ARM. However, it is time to examine QEMU.

Virtual machine configuration

You can as well proceed with the setting of your VM with the download of your Linux operating system. When prompted, input your email address as you begin to launch VMware Workstation Player. Getting the software for free is what this aspect is all about, and the email list of the VMware gets you on board. The primary application of VMware Workstation Player will load when you have completed that level. And to proceed, your virtual machine will require the creation of an account. The ISO, installer disc image file is the default that you will choose. Note that there is an option of installing the OS later by merely having a blank disk to create a virtual system. Then, you will click "Next" after the installation of your preferred operating system. Your chosen guest OS will install automatically as a message about the installation of VMware Easy Install.

Account creation

Your password, username, and the preferred name are all the information you will enter in the next screen and then hit the "next" button when you name your VM. For the operating system that you are installing, what most times follow its name is the default, and also for your VM, you may go ahead and choose a location. Hit the "next" button again, and you will select the disk capacity for your VM. As a series of files or a file for the physical disk of your computer, this is a saved virtual hard disk. Either option is there for you to select. Meanwhile, you can either alter or accept a recommended size used for your virtual HDD. It could be more than striking because increasing tends to be a safer option. Hit the "next" button again, whatever your choice to come to a screen with "ready to create the virtual machine." Hit on the "finish' button, and the VM will start. So far, after creation, run your virtual machine. Soon, you get the suggestion for the tools of VMware for Linux package, which will arrive through an alert. As an approach to the Easy Installation process, this may not be that necessary. But it's fine when you accept this.

Virtual hardware customization

The customize hardware is another option on the screen for "ready to create..." Now, in another way beyond the HDD, you may want to tweak the hardware of the virtual machine. There are so many options you can choose from, including network adaptor configuration, processors, and memory. You may want to check out the screen of Processors. You will come across a reference to a Virtualization engine in the right-hand pane. This process is already in Automatic by default. As such, indeed, for Linux, you may not have to worry about anything. However, you can set this to Intel VT-x or other alternatives if you run into any problems. Then, in the Memory screen, you can deal with specific issues of performance. Here, also, as a recommended maximum and minimum for your virtual machine, you can see the diagram of the suggested size of RAM. Stick to these recommendations as it tends to be ideal. You may likely slow everything from running the VM software to standard system tasks with the impact on your PC performance when you set the Ram too high, and you will still have issues at hand by going too small.

Ultimately, your settings for display will require a bit of your time. Here, you can decide to set up multiple monitors in your virtual machine or utilize the host computer's monitor settings since you will have the ability to toggle 3D acceleration. There will be a display of a recommended amount as with system memory for the guest operating system, and you can also adjust the graphics memory.

Using Linux in VMware Workstation Player after installation

On a physical desktop machine, it is typical of the operating system installed in the virtual machine to boot the ISO. You can go ahead and automate the entire process through the method of Easy Install, and to apply for setting in the guest, the virtual OS, you can use your Windows host OS configuration. It is useful to pay attention here because you can have the overall control over the operating system installation if you chose the option to install the OS later. Then, you can begin to use the guest OS since you will have access to log into the virtual machine when the installation is complete with the use of Easy Install. As simple as that! Subsequently, with the menu where your virtual machine can be opened, you can also launch the VM.

The Importance of Virtual Machine

For Linux, hardware happened to be a significant encounter in 2005. People were having different issues with USB devices, graphics, Bluetooth, and even wireless. And to make things work, you might have to find wrappers and drivers all the time a new invention came people's way. Since the virtual machine appeared not to be the option, and for any user of Linux to identify the solution, they must interact with the 'real' hardware. However, there have been so many changes. On Linux, a handful of hardware works unplanned. There has been a shift in the focus on the distributions' unique features with less essence on the support for hardware. You can write about them on a similar machine if you can easily play with multiple distributions, and you are a virtual machines' heavy user.

Now, for new users of Linux and the ways they can take advantage of them, let's discuss some benefits of virtual machines even though in the enterprise segment, virtual machines are used extensively.

Who needs to use a virtual machine?

Since there is no availability of specific proprietary services and software, some users of Linux have to boot in twofold. And there is only support for Windows concerning tax filling software as well as some related works by the government in many countries. For you to run Windows software, you can easily use a virtual machine instead of working through the pain and complexity of dual booting. Then, it is only on gaming that the virtual machines may not function. Mainly when you are playing resource-hungry games such as Crysis, to have the desired gaming experience, you may need to talk to real RAM, GPU, and CPU. Since between the hardware and the application, you may not like a virtual layer, video, and audio editing may not work either. Virtual machines work great outside of these and even a few other capacities.

Also, by switching to Linux or formatting the operating system they were used to or playing with Linux, for the individuals that attempt to make a change as non-Linux users, a virtual machine may also be useful. When they are ready, they will have the self-assurance to make the shift since virtual machines get these individuals comfortable with Linux. As such, inside your Windows 10 or Mac OS, you can be running Linux. Above all, to switch between distributions without having to reboot on the same hardware, you can run multiple Linux distributions on virtual machines. Instead of entirely dependent on anyone or being vendor-locked, you will need to be versed with several major distributions as a Linux user. And without having to log out to change the environment, on the same system, you may similarly run various desktop backgrounds with the use of virtual machines. You may not know the type of operating system your client or employer would be using. Thus, in any Linux, you will need some knowledge because you certainly don't want to know only one distribution if you're aspiring to become a developer or system admin. And for testing your applications, you will require several distributions if you are a developer.

As you can see now, working with virtual machines has several advantages. Also, operating virtualization has some significant benefits, which is efficiency, apart from multi-booting. Switching between different distributions and having hard drives formatted can be a waste of your time. So, it is as simple as starting the latest application, and without affecting your work, you can begin a new virtual machine for distribution with virtual machines. A virtual machine can be bliss if you are an enthusiast or distribution-hopper. Keep your attention on several other distributions such as Linux Mint, Fedora, Ubuntu, Kubuntu, OpenSUSE, and so many others even if you are an Arch Linux user. As it takes up space and misuse of financial means, having several physical systems can be virtually impossible. It pays to make a good investment in some multicore processor and more RAM, which can run additional virtual systems than buying six physical machines. Now, you won't experience any form of downtime if, on the same machines, you handle nearly a dozen distributions.

The types of virtual machines to use

You have some alternatives, including VirtualBox, Xen, KVM, Qemu, VMware, and so much more. Others have their advantages and also their disadvantages. Though, solutions such as KVM tend to be quite efficient and more powerful even if you have a preference for VirtualBox. As a new user of Linux, you will find the ease of use of the VirtualBox. And without technical know-how that can be quite hard-core, you can access its tons of functionalities and features. Since VirtualBox can be installed on Mac, Windows, and Linux, and the support for cross-platform is its most significant advantage.

Chapter 5: Linux User Management and System Administration

In computing technology, the major strength is Linux. Linux powers several of the cloud-servers, supercomputers, personal computers, mobile phones, and webservers. In addition to using command-line interface tools and Linux tools to take backups, creating, enhancing, and maintaining user reports or accounts, managing the operations of a computer system is the job of a Linux systems administrator. Linux powers most of the computing devices because of its open-source environment, high security, and high stability. It is essential to know and understand the specific qualities of an administrator of a Linux system:

- Handling users, directories, and file

- Basic bash command

- Managing superuser or root

- Files system hierarchy

- Linux file systems

A Linux administrator's duties

For an institute or organization that needs an excellent IT foundation, a reliable criterion is the system administrator. Hence, all-time requirements will be the need for efficient Linux administrators. As there may be additional duties and responsibilities to the role, from each organization, the job profile might change. Here are a few responsibilities of a Linux administrator:

- During an issue with the server, it is the job of the administrator to troubleshoot.

- Essential security tools and system installation. To make necessary recommendations after analyzing hardware requirements, the administrator works with the data network engineer and other departments or personnel.

- Ranging from login issues to disaster recovery, Linux administrator detects and solves the service problems.

- For the Linux environments and its users, creating, maintaining, and enhancing the required tools.

- One of the characters of a Linux administrator is to communicate at all times in a professional, cultivated manner with customers, vendors, and staff.

- Apart from offering excellent customer support for ISP, web hosting, and LAN customers about troubleshooting all increased support troubles, Linux administrator also fixes and analyzes all error logs.

- Part of the duties is listing backup, creating new stored procedures, and taking regular backup of data.

- Internet request maintenance, such as PHP, MySQL, Apache, RADIUS, and DNS.

Linux system admin career process

- Learn how to install and use Linux environment

- Have Linux administration certification

- Become an expert in documentation

- Look for help and support by joining community or group of a local Linux users

Necessarily, taking backup and managing the operations, such as examining hardware and software systems, are a few roles of the Linux systems administrator. Also, the admin must be able to describe technical knowledge understanding quite profoundly.

How to Manage Users and Groups as a Linux Administrator

All at the same time, more than one user can make use of Linux since it is a multi-user operating system. And to manage users in a system, Linux offers a beautiful mechanism. Therefore, getting along with the groups and users in a system is the most significant function of a system administrator. And we will use the CentOS Linux distribution to talk about all the commands used below.

Linux user

The unique identification number, UID, is a binary number that uniquely identifies an account of a user of a system. Normal users and super or root user are the two types of users. There will be limited access to files for the regular users while there will be full access to all the data for super or root user. A user account can be modified, deleted, or added by a superuser. It is in the /etc/passwd/ file that the full account information is stored and also on the /etc/shadow/ file that a hash password is stored.

Using a default setting to create a user

At the command prompt, by running the useradd command, a user can be added. Use passwd utility to set a password after creating the user like this:

```
[root@localhost handy32]# useradd enirban

[root@localhost handy32]# passwd anirban

Changing password for user anirban.

New password:
```

40

Retype new password:

passwd: all authentication tokens updated successfully.

There will be an automatic setting of the default shell to */bin/bash,* creation of the home directory *(/home/<username>),* and the assigning of a UID by the system. Anytime the system has added to it a new user and also uses the user name for the group, a user private group is created by the *useradd* command. When a user is created, specify the full name of the user. For the specification of the full name of the user, use *useradd* with the option *-c* as a system administrator:

[root@localhost   handy32]#   useradd   -c   "Anirban Choudhury" handy32

Using UID to create a user

Using the *-u* option and a custom UID, a user can be created like this:

[root@localhost handy32]# useradd -u 1036 handy32

Using the home directory with a non-default to create a user

By doing the below, you can set a home directory with a non-default:

[root@localhost handy32]# useradd -d /home/test handy32

Having user added to a supplementary group and primary group

Through the specification of the *-G* and *-g* option, it is possible to specify a complementary group and the primary one as an administrator.

```
[root@loaclhost    handy32]#    useradd    -g    "head"    -G
"faculty" handy32
```

User lock and unlock

A user account can be locked or unlocked by a superuser.
Using the option $-/$, you only have to invoke *passwd* to lock
an account.

```
[root@localhost handy32]# passwd -/ handy32
For user handy32, Locking password
passwd: Success
```

To unlock an account, you can use *passwd* and the $-u$ option:

```
[root@localhost handy32]#  passwd -u handy32
For user handy32 to unlock password
passwd: Success
```

Changing username

For username login change, use *usermod* command with the
$-/$ option:

```
[root@localhost handy32]# usermod -/ "nishant" handy32
```

User removal

Using the home directory and a user with the combination of
the $-r$ option and *userdel*:

```
[root@loaclhost handy32]# userdel -r handy32
```

Linux Group

A mechanism used for the collection and organization of users
is the Linux group. The group ID, GID, is a uniquely
associated ID for each group, like the user ID. We have the
supplementary and primary groups as the two types of groups.
The primary group belongs to each user and of zero or more

42

than zero complementary groups. It is in /etc/group/ that the information of the group is stored and also in the /etc/gshadow file that the respective passwords are stored.

Using the default setting to create a group

As a root user, run the groupadd command with the default settings to add a new group:

```
[root@localhost handy32]# groupadd employee
```

Using the group name, type gpasswd if you want to add a password:

```
[root@localhost handy32]# gpasswd employee
For group employee, changing the password
New Password:
Re-enter new password:
```

Using a specified GID to create a group

With the use of the -g option, execute the groupadd command to specify the group's GID explicitly:

```
[root@loaclhost handy32]# groupadd -g 1200 manager
```

Group password removal

Using the proper group name, run gpasswd -r to remove a group password:

```
[root@loaclhost handy32]# gpasswd -r employee
```

Changing the name of the group

As a superuser, use the -n option as you run the groupmod command to change the name of the group:

```
[root@loacalhost handy32]# groupmod -n hrsupervisor employee
```

Changing the GID of the group

Along with `-g`, run the `groupmod` command to change the group's GID:

```
[root@loaclhost handy32]# groupmod -g 1050 manager
```

Deleting a group

You will first need to delete the users of that primary group before you can delete a primary group. With the group name, run the `groupdel` command to delete a group:

```
[root@loaclhost handy32]# groupdel employee
```

The File System of Linux

The technique of storing files on a hard disk is a file system. And Linux supports several types of file systems including:

- Special-purpose file systems: debugfs, tmpfs, sysfs, procfs, etc.

- Flash storage file systems: YAFFS, JFFS2, ubifs, etc.

- Conventional disk file systems: NTFS, JFS, Btrfs, XFS, ext4, ext3, ext2, etc.

The hierarchy standard of the file system

The file system hierarchy is a standard layout used to store files for the Linux system. Here are some directory structures for the most common Linux:

The online manual page for Linux

There is a help or support for every single command for Linux, and this is one of the key features of Linux. You will have to type the following command for the manual page of the Linux to be accessed:

```
[handy32@localhost~]$man /s
```

44

The command page of the manual will be provided when you do this.

Root or superuser

For anyone to do any alteration to a service or program of Linux with access to all kinds of permission, this account is a special kind of user account. To become root or superuser, you will use the su command and to become one, all you have to do is to enter the root password by typing the following command:

```
[handy32@localhost~]$su
```

Directories and files handling

Everything is a file inside Linux. As such, through file operation related commands, there's an interaction with them during the time of dealing with device files or standard text files. Below are a few operations on the files:

File creation:

For the creation of a file, two commands are quite necessary, and they are cat and $touch$. To create an empty file, you can make use of the $touch$ by following the example below:

```
[handy32@loaclhost~]$touch file1
```

To view or create a file, you will use the cat which you do by following this step:

```
[handy32@loacalhost~]$cat>file1
```

Also, you can use the command below to view a file type:

```
[handy32@localhost~]$cat file1
```

Copying a file:

For you to copy a file from one location to another, you can use the `cp` command like this:

```
[handy32@localhost~]$cp file1 /home/sandra/Documents/
```

The current working directory will be copied by this command to `/home/bhargab/Documents/`.

Removing a file:

You can type the command below to remove a file:

```
[handy32@localhost~]$rm file1
```

Moving or renaming a file:

To rename or move a file; the command you can use is the `mv`. Use below command to move a file from one place to another:

```
[handy32@loaclhost~]$mv file /home/sandra/Document
```

Under `/home/sandra/`, the Document directory will get the file1 with the use of the above command. Then, from file1 to file2, you can perform the below command to rename a file.

```
[handy32@loaclhost~]$mv file1 file2
```

Directories and files listing:

The contents are the `ls` lists, which are directories and files of the specified directory or current directory. For the contents of the current directory to be displayed, use the below command:

```
[handy32@localhost~]$ls
```

46

The directory name, as well as the file name, will be listed by this command. You can use the command below to list all files in the hidden files and also your home directory:

```
[handy32@localhost~]$ls □a
```

With the / option, type `ls` to view files in a long-listing format:

```
[handy32@localhost~]$ls □l
```

Below, you will see a portion of the output:

```
Total of 48

drwxr-xr-x. 2 handy32 handy32 4096 Jan 25 21:32
Desktop
drwxr-xr-x. 2 handy32 handy32 4096 Apr 24 16:33
Documents
drwxr-xr-x. 6 handy32 handy32 4096 Jan 20 23:55
Downloads
-rw-rw-r--. 1 handy32 handy32   1024 Apr 28 22:18
file1
-rw-rw-r--. 1 handy32 handy32   1024 Apr 28 22:01
file2
-rw-rw-r--. 1 handy32 handy32   1024 Apr 28 22:01
file3
drwxr-xr-x. 2 handy32 handy32 4096 Dec 20 08:48 Music
drwxr-xr-x. 2 handy32 handy32 4096 Dec 20 08:48
Pictures
drwxr-xr-x. 2 handy32 handy32 4096 Dec 20 08:48
Public
drwxr-xr-x. 2 handy32 handy32 4096 Dec 20 08:48
Videos
```

48 is the total number of disk blocked, as indicated by the total 48. In each of the lines, there are nine columns, and the following permission was represented by each column, including file name, time and date, bytes sizes, group name, and numbers of links. There are 10 subfields in the permission field, and the type of file is what the first field represents. The (u) permission denotes the next three fields, while the representations of the group (g) permissions are

47

the seventh, sixth, and fifth fields. The (o) permissions have its representation in the last three fields with read permission from (r), execute permission from (x), and write permission from (w).

The soft and hard links

In the hard disk, a connection between the actual data and a file name is a link, and these, are soft and hard links. When you follow the command below, you can create a hard link:

```
[handy32@loaclhost~]$ln file1 file2
```

And by following the command below, create a soft link:

```
[handy32@localhost~]$ln □S file1 file3
```

Changing Mod:

For every file in Linux, there are three types of connected permission, and they are (x) for execute, (w) for write, and (r) for read. Through the superuser or the owner of the file, it is easy to change the existing file permission. To embed a `write` permission to the group, use the command below:

```
[handy32@localhost~]$chmod g+w file1
```

Also, use the following command for other users to have an execute permission:

```
[handy32@localhost~]$chmod o+x file1
```

You may use the following the command below when you want to take away execute permission from a group:

```
[handy32@localhost~]$chmod g-x file1
```

Current working directory

Below, you will see the display of the current working directory through the *pwd* command:

```
[sandrahandy32@localhost~]$pwd
/home/sandra
```

As such, the */home/sandra/* is the current working directory.

Directory creation:

For the creation of a directory, you can use the *mkdir* command like this:

```
[sandrahandy32@localhost~]$mkdir myDir
```

Under */home/sandra/*, a directory will be created.

Directory removal:

For an empty directory to be removed, you will use the *rmdir* command like this:

```
[sandrahandy32@localhost~]$rmdir MyDir
```

You will also remove the parent directories and not only the specified directory with the *p* option using *rmdir*.

```
[handy32@localhost~]$rmdir □ p myDir.
```

So far, we have covered extensively so many angles on the system administration and also Linux user management. You may want to go back and read through them for some time to get abreast of some of the things discussed in this segment. When you do, you can get over to the next section, where we will go in-depth on Linux directory structures.

Chapter 6: Linux Directory Structures

There are needs for data storage on an HDD, hard disk of several types, or a few similarities, including a USB for every general-purpose computer. These needs come with a couple of reasons. In the first place, anytime you switch off your computer, the contents of the RAM can be lost. And as for the use of solid-state drives and USB memory sticks, after the removal of power, the maintenance of the stored data in them tends to be the function of non-volatile RAM types. Quite expensive is the flash RAM than other related categories like the volatile, standard RAM such as DDR3. The disk space is not as expensive as the standard RAM because the data storage by hard drives tends to be the second reason. Regarding per byte cost, RAM is still more useful. There's been a rapid drop in the value of both disk and RAM. As per unit, the hard drive is about 71 times less expensive the RAM, based on a 2TB hard drive costs against 16GB of RAM as a quick calculation of the cost per byte.

In a few confusing and different ways, there are a lot of discussions from several quarters about filesystems. With regards to the perspective of a document or analysis, you will need to distinguish the exact meaning since the word itself can have multiple meanings. For using it in distinctive conditions and based on people's observations, let's attempt to define several meanings of the term 'filesystem.' The intention is to make this definition grounded on its several handlings as we strive to adapt to the conventional official meanings.

1. With a specific kind of filesystem, a formatted logical or partition volume that, on a Linux filesystem, can be mounted on a specified point.

2. A particular formatted data storage like XFS, BTRFS, EXT4, EXT#, EXT2, etc. 100 filesystems types have support on Linux, including the newest in addition to the oldest. And to define accessing and storing the data,

50

these filesystem varieties function by its metadata structures.

3. The start of the entire Linux directory structure is at the top (/) root directory.

Basic functions of the filesystem

There are specific inescapable and exciting details that the disk storage encompasses with it as a necessity. Essentially, the provision of non-volatile data storage is one of the ultimate functions and purposes of a filesystem. However, from that requirement, there are some other essential functions. The provision of a namespace is what the whole filesystems have to execute; a methodology of organizational and naming. And out of the entire set of characters available, this process defines the manner with which you can brand a file, particularly the subset of characters and the length of a filename that you can use in place of filenames. Also, atop a disk, the data's logical structure is what it defines, including limping files in a vast, single conglomeration as well as for organizing files with the directories usage. For the provision of that namespace's rational base, quite necessary is the structure of metadata when the namespace has been defined. As such, for the support of a classified directory structure, there is an obligatory addition of data structures. These structures make the determination of the used space blocks upon the disk as well as those available. As for the maintenance of the directories' names and files, the structures that allow that and also the statistics about the data position or locations which, on the disk, belong to the folder, last accessed or modified, as well as times and sizes they were created. For the storing of the sophisticated material of the disk's subdivisions, they make use of other metadata, including logical partitions and volumes. It represents the structures and more complex metadata, which, separated and independent of the filesystem metadata, confine the data expressing the filesystem accumulated on the partition or drive.

Also, for the provision of access to the function of the system calls that control filesystem objects such as directories and files, API, Application Programming Interface is also required for filesystems. The tasks of deleting, moving, and creating files are provided by the APIs. Including the location on a filesystem that you place a file, part of the things APIs offer is algorithms that determine things. For minimizing and speeding the disk fragmentation, objectives may be the purpose of such algorithms. As a pattern for rights of entry definition to directories and files, there is also a security model in the place provided by modern filesystems. As a user, you can have a way into other people's files or the OS as a result of the Linux filesystem security model. For the implementation of these purposes, the required software is the ultimate building block. And as a technique to enhance programmer efficiency and both system, the application of two-part software is what Linux uses. The virtual filesystem of Linux is this implementation's first part of the two. For the access to the filesystems of all types and also the provision of a single command set for the developers and the kernel is done by this virtual filesystem. And the driver of the specific required device to interface gets a call from the virtual filesystem software to the several kinds of filesystems. The second section of the execution is the drivers of the filesystem-exclusive appliance. On the logical or partition volume and to those explicit to the types of the filesystem, the filesystem commands' standard set is interpreted by the device driver.

Directory Structure of Linux

The file system structure of Linux can appear particularly alien if you are the type that is coming from Windows. Now mostly with three-letter names, the cryptic-sounding directories and a / option have replaced the forgotten drive letters as well as the C : \ drive. What defines some other Unix-related OS and the structure of file systems on Linux is the FHS, Filesystem Hierarchy Standard. However, also contained in the Linux filesystems are some directories that are not yet defined by the standard.

/var – Variable Data Files

As it must be read-only in the usual operation, the writable counterpart to the /usr directory is the /var directory. During normal operation, we can write to the /var directory the log files as well as all things else that would normally be written to /usr. For example, in /var/log, the log file can be found there.

/usr – Read-Only Data & User Binaries

Contrary to files and applications that the system uses, users use files and applications that contain the directory /usr. For example, rather than the directory /sbin, the location of the non-elemental binaries of the system administration, the location of non-essential applications is within the directory /usr/bin. There are other directories contained in the /usr directory, including architecture-free folder such as graphics which share location in /usr/. This process prevents them from mucking up the rest of the system, where the local directory usr/ is, by default, found installed in the locally assembled applications.

/tmp – Temporary Files

Whenever your system is restarted, since it is in the /tmp directory where application stored temporary files, the utilities like tmpwatch will have these files deleted at any time.

/srv – Service data

The 'data for services provided by the system' is contained by the /srv directory. You would probably store the files of your website in a directory inside the /srv directory if you were using the Apache HTTP server to serve a website.

/selinux SELinux Virtual File System

With SELinux, the directory /selinux contains special files if, for security purposes, Red Hat and Fedora use SELinux by your Linux distribution. It is the same as the /proc. On Ubuntu, this folder's presence appears to be a bug since Ubuntu doesn't use SELinux.

/sbin – System Administration Binaries

The directory /bin is parallel to the directory /sbin. And for system administration, it is generally intended to be run by the root user as it contains essential binaries.

/run – State Files Application

For the requirement, such as process IDs and sockets, to store transient place, the directory /run gives a standard place application as it is fairly new. Since files in /tmp may be deleted, /tmp can't store these files.

/root – Home Directory for Root

The home directory for the root operator is the directory /root. As the system root directory, its location is at /root instead of /home/root for the location.

/proc – Kernel & Process Files

Since it doesn't contain standard files, the directory /dev is the same as the /proc directory. Special files to process and represent information are all that it contains.

/opt – Optional Packages

For optional software packages, these directories are contained in the directory /opt. Since the standard filesystem hierarchy doesn't have its respect, the proprietary software commonly uses it. For instance, as you install it, it might dump the files of proprietary programs in /opt/application.

/mnt – Transitory Mount Points

While using them, where the temporary filesystems are mounted by the system administrator is the directory /mnt. For example, for the execution of a few operations of file recovery, you may well want to mount a partition on windows /mnt/ for Windows if you are mounting it. However, to mount other system files, you may choose any space on the system.

/media – Removable Media

Where the devices inserted into the computer are mounted is where subdirectories contain the /media directory. For instance, a directory will automatically be created inside the /media directory as you insert a CD into your Linux system. And inside this directory, you can access the contents of the CD.

/lost+found – Recovered Files

There is a `lost+found` directory in each filesystem of Linux. As such, a filesystem check will be performed at the next boot if the filesystem crashes. And for the extensive recovery of data, it is in the `lost+found` directory will any corrupted files found be placed.

/lib – Essential Shared Libraries

In the /sbin and /bin directories, required essential binaries are contained libraries in the /lib directory. Binaries needed by libraries within a /usr/bin folder are located within /usr/lib.

/home – Home Files

For each user, the directory /home contains a file for home. For example, /home/greg will be the location for the home folder if your username is Greg. User-explicit formation file and user's data files are contained in this home folder. On the system, for you to have other files modified as the superuser, each user needs to obtain elevated permission even when they only have the write access to their home folder.

/etc. – Configuration Files

Though easily edited by hand in a text editor, the maintenance of the configuration files is contained by the /etc. directory. Be aware that the system-wide configuration files are contained by the /etc/ directory, and it is in each home directory of the user that user-specific configuration files are located.

/dev – Devices Files

As files, devices are exposed by Linux. As such, devices that have the representation of some special files are the directory /dev. Though they seem like files, much known to us, we can't call them original files. For instance, in the system, the major SATA drive is represented by the /dev/sda. For you to inform it to edit /dev/sda, you could begin a compartment editor if you want to partition it as virtual devices without any hardware correlation. Also, pseudo-devices are contained in this directory. For example, there are only random numbers that the /dev/random produces. As it creates no output, an exceptional device is /dev/null that instinctively have all inputs discarded when, toward /dev/ null, a command's output is piped.

/cdrom – CD-ROMs Historical Mount Point

A directory that doesn't belong to the standard of FHS is the directory /cdrom. However, when you go to Ubuntu and other OS, you will find it. For CD-ROMs inserted in the system, it is a temporary location. However, it is inside the /media directory for the standard location of temporary media.

/boot – Static Boot Files

The files needed to boot the system is contained by the /boot directory. For example, stored here are your Linux kernels and the GRUB boot loader's files. Though their location with other files is in the /etc directory, the configuration files of the boot loader are not located here.

/bin – Essential User Binaries

When the system is mounted in a single-user mode, the essential user binaries, otherwise known as programs that must be present, are contained within the /bin directory. It is in /usr/bin that applications like Firefox is stored, while the location for vital utilities and system programs like bash shell are in /bin directory. You can also store in another partition the /usr directory. Though, even if no other filesystems are mounted, you will be sure to have these essential utilities when you place these files in the /bin directory. As it contains crucial binaries for system administration, similar to it is the /sbin directory.

/ - the Root Directory

Known as the root directory, it is under the / directory that you can locate everything on the Linux system. On Windows, the C:\ directory is quite similar to / directory. However, since Linux doesn't have drive letters, this is not strictly true. On Windows, while D:\ is the location for another partition, on Linux, it is in another folder under / directory that other partition would appear.

Chapter 7: Working with Disk, Media, and Data Files (gzip – tar)

Before you can use them, you must structure storage devices like USB drives and hard drives since the regular practice in Linux is deleting and creating partitions. *Partitions* often host separate sections of devices with considerable storage after they have been divided. Also, you can divide into isolated parts of the hard drive using the partitions where, as a discrete hard drive, each section behaves as such. If you administer several OS, partitioning can be particularly useful. In Linux, otherwise known as disk partition manipulation, you can remove or create this with the use of several powerful tools. As such, devices with large disk can benefit as well as several disk partitions, and we will go in-depth on how to use the `parted` command. Here are some common commands like `cfdisk` and `fdisk`, as well as the difference between `parted`.

- **Reliability**: in a DOS partition, only one copy of the partition table is stored. At the end and the beginning of the disk, two copies of the partition table are kept by the GPT. Also, done with DOS partitions to check the partition table integrity, the GPT uses a CRC checksum.

- **More partitions**: it is only 16 partitions that the tables of DOS partition permit with the use of extended and primary partitions. Having many more is what you can choose and by default, can get up to 128 partitions with GPT.

- **Larger disks**: in some cases, up to 16TB is possible even though a partition of the DOS table tends to format up to 2TB of disk space. However, up to 8ZiB of space can be addressed by a GPT partition table.

58

- **GPT format**: while, to DOS partition tables, `cfdisk` and `fdisk` are limited, a Globally Unique Identifiers Partition Table, GPT can be created by the `parted` command.

It is recommended to use `parted` to function with disk partitions because working with them will require more flexibility in today's larger disks. Most often, part of the operating system installation process is the creation of the disk partition. When an existing system is getting an addition of a storage device, direct use of the `parted` command is most useful.

Analyze Disk Space and Hard Disk Partition on Linux with These Commands

For you to check the partitions on your systems, there are some commands you can use. Part of what the commands might do is checking what partitions exist on every floppy disk and some additional details such as filesystem, consumed space, total size, so many others. Though they can also modify them, there are some tools for partitioning where the partition material can be displayed, including `cfdisk`, `sfdisk`, and `fdisk`.

hwinfo

You can make use of `hwinfo` to print out the partition and disk list, as a general-purpose hardware information tool. However, like the other commands, the output doesn't print details about each partition.

blkid

Though it doesn't report the space on the partitions, `blkid` prints the block devices, storage and partitions media, attributes such as `uuid` and file system type.

lsblk

Optical drives and disk partitions, as well as all the storage blocks, are listed out by `lsblk`. If any, it lists out the mount point and, most notably, the total size of the block/partition. On the partitions, free/used space is not reported. It indicates that the filesystem is not yet mounted if there is no MOUNTPOINT. Also, it means that there is no disk for DVD/CD. With a device such as the model and label, `lsblk` is capable of displaying more information.

pydf

Written in Python is the improved version of `pydf`, and in an easy to read manner, it prints out all the hard disk partitions. Also, it is only the mounted file systems that `pydf` is limited to show.

df

This command prints out details about only mounted filesystems even though it is not a partitioning utility. Even filesystems that are not real disk partitions are some of the list generated by `df`. When you use it, you will discover that the actual partitions or devices are only the file systems that start with a `/dev`, and to filter out the real hard disk partitions or filesystems, you can use `grep`. Then, use `df` to display only actual disk partitions with the type of partition.

parted

If needed, this modifies the list as it also lists out the partitions being another command-line utility.

cfdisk

Based on `ncurses` with an interactive user interface, the partition editor of Linux is `cfdisk`. Use it to modify or create current partitions in addition to listing out those partitions. One partition can only run at a time with `cfdisk`, and as such, pass the device name to `cfdisk` if the details of a specific disk are required.

sfdisk

In addition to a goal similar to `fdisk`, however, with additional features, another utility is `sfdisk`. Each partition's size can be displayed in MB.

fdisk

For the checking of the partition on a disk, the most commonly used command is the `fdisk`. Like filesystem type, you can get the display of the partitions and details with the use of the `fdisk` command. However, each partition size report may not be available with `fdisk`.

Linux Data Manipulation

It can be confusing with the Linux world if you are the type that is quite used to Windows. What with no image, link, or anything to click, few hints, no wizards, and so on. And also, before anything can be done, you need to know what it is you want. Let's assume that, somehow contrary to your interest, you have no choice but to use the shell prompt of Linux and learning the agonizing, cryptic program where the xkcd forms its basis does not tally with your burning desire. However, for the processing of your data, the use of the command-line might have in it some good reasons. Attempting to make use of Excel to deal with this data may not be suitable even with the new technologies offering digital data terabytes and more instruments providing a digital output. You may not also get anywhere near luck with the use of CSV files. However, with the use of free, reasonably simple utilities on Linux, these can be easily managed. Also, another reason for taking this path is that the powerful mainstream tools for Linux come with no cost.

Though we may want to leave out most of these, however, SAS, Mathematica, MATLAB, and so on have been ported to Linux and are a few excellent branded tools. As it works better on Linux and as second nature on Linux, we may not imply that using native applications and utilities may not do well on Windows. Also, there is a constant assurance that on Linux, it will work always. Since there's a payment option for Apple and Microsoft in money and time by releasing yet another pointless upgrade to bump their profit, you don't need to learn a new interface every 6 months.

Identifying the file type

It is possible you are not aware of the kind of data it is even though the data might have been generated in the lab. The file is a device that can proffer some help even though it is not foolproof. The response it tends to give comes from the question: "what file type is it?" If there are any diagnostic characteristics, file peeks inside the file to see them, unlike the endings of the file name mapping approach of Windows, which has filename.typ to a specific type. And it can be quite helpful suppose there's been name-mangled or renamed in translation to the file.

Hypotheses

With the installation of Linux standard famous utilities, including R, the hypothesis is that on a Linux, you have access to a bash shell. For this exercise, a directory can be created. For DataDir, it is quite on $DDIR$ that you can give it your reference, though you can give it any name you like. And to the DDIR variable of the shell, you may as well have actual term assigned to it:

Export DDIR=/stephen/leo/

bash> is the prefix of the shell commands and to test your shell, including comments with embed (with # as a prefix; you may as well ignore them) can mouse into it. Also, you may want to ignore the prefix bash>. Also, at the UC Irvine and on the cluster nodes of the interactive BDUC, accessible here are all the defined utilities. And for any Linux distribution, you can get them without any costs, except they state otherwise.

The size of the file

`red+blue all.txt.gz`, a tab-bordered data file of 25MB is what we are going to use. By pressing upon the link with a right-clicking, you can download it in Firefox and hit 'save.' For this exercise, use the directory `$DDIR` to save it. Then, use `gunzip blue+red_all.txt.gz` to decompress it. After that, with `ls`, the result of the entire bytes will be achieved.

Using Linux to Mount and Unmount Media

With the use of the operating system of a Linux, you can have media mounted and unmounted with this process. You must be aware that the default Red Hat installation is what this process uses, and thus, with the use of other Linux operating system types, the commands, structures, and file names might not be the same. Now, let's get down to the business!

If you are mounting a CD, follow the steps below:

1. Ensure that, on your server, there is a presence of the `/nt/cdrom` directory. You can type `mkdir/mnt/cdrom` if there's no existence of this directory. Then, hit the 'enter' button.

2. Then, have `mount/dev/scd0 -t iso9660 -o ro /mnt/cdrom` typed for you to mount the CD. Again, hit the 'enter' button.

If the disk is the instrument you want to mount, you can follow the below command:

1. Be certain that on the server, you have `/mnt/floppy` directory. You may want to type the below command if there's no existence of this directory:

    `mkdir/mnt/disk`

Again, hit the 'enter' button.

2. You can type the following command to have the disk mounted:

```
mount/dev/sda -o auto/mnt/disk
```

Then, hit the 'enter' button.

For you to unmount the media, you can follow the command below:

1. Input CD and hit enter.

2. Follow the commands below:

- You can type the command below if it is your CD that you want to unmount:

```
unmounts /mnt/cdrom
```

Then, hit the 'enter' button.

- You can type the command below if it is a disk that you want to unmounts:

```
unmounts mnt/floppy
```

Again, hit the 'enter' button.

Creating from the Command-line a File for Tar GZip

If you are managing your backups away from Time Machine or you want to have file groups transferred, having the zip files made could have been something you are probably doing. The command line can be an excellent option for you to make a gzip and tar archive if you prefer better compression and also additional advanced options using the user-friendly and accessible tools of GUI zip. And typical of Linux elements, even in Mac OS X, the syntax will be similar.

Bundle creation the archive of tar gzip

You can make use of the syntax from the (terminal/applications/) command-line. For example, you could have jpg files directories compressed by typing some specific commands.

Here, a wildcard is the *, which means that you can have .jpe compressed from any file that has the extension .jpg, and that is all. Though offering compression on its own, tar packages become a bundle of a single file from a set of files as two distinctive products are the resulting `.tar.gz.` file. Therefore, gzip compression is quite valuable to supplement for you to have the tar compressed. And if you want it, you can have them as different commands while running them. However, as you can automatically have the tar file gzipped since the flag `-z` is what tar command offers, there is no much need for it.

Chapter 8: File, Directory Manager, Permissions, Networking, and SSH

As a layer generally, the operating system that handles your data positioning on the storage is any filesystem on Linux. And even if you discover any unsupported filesystem type, you will not know which file starts where and what files end where without it. For software that can deal with it, you may even download it. As such, what are the Linux filesystem types? You will notice that Linux provides several filesystems such as the ones below when you attempt to install it: swap, btrfs, jfs, ext4, ext3, ext2, ext

Therefore, what are these filesystems that Linux provides?

Btrfs

Oracle made this one, and in some distributions, it is not entirely stable as Ext. However, if you have to, you may think that it is a replacement for it, and it has excellent performance.

XFS

Using it with small files, it works slowly being an old filesystem

JFS

IBM made this old filesystem and, whether, with big or small files, it works quite well. However, after a long time, as indicated by reports, it failed, and files get corrupted.

Ext4

With a significant speed, this gives room for large files. If you are looking for an option for SSD disk, you may want to go for this, and it is the suggested default filesystem you will see when you want to install Linux.

Ext3

With backward compatibility and upgrades, it comes with Ext2. And since this filesystem doesn't give any support for

66

disk snapshots or file recovery, servers no longer use this type of filesystem.

Ext2

This gives room for 2 terabytes of data allowed as the Linux first filesystem.

Ext

Because of limitations, people are no longer using this old one.

High-Level Explanation

Now is the time to know from the high-level, what is inside those filesystems since you are familiar with the Linux filesystem. If you are someone coming from Windows, it will be possible to install partitions such as D:\ and C:\, usually C:\, because Windows has partitions like them. Though we have discussed it in some previous chapter, what is the filesystem structure of Linux? You will see the Linux filesystem hierarchy when you navigate to the root partition, which is /.

Linux Directory Management Commands

For us to translate between IP addresses and domain names, the domain name system, DNS, is what we utilize. For example, on a Linux system, for DNS hookup, you may use the host command or dig command. Similarly, it is not by inode number but by file names that people refer to Linux files. As such, what is the directory's actual function? It is according to your usage that you tend to group the files. For example, you can do that under /etc/ directory that all configuration files are stored. Thus, making a connection between the file names and their connected inode number is the purpose of a directory. And you will discover two sub-directories inside every directory named:

1. .. (double period) – the pointer to the previous directory, i.e., the directory above the one you are in at present. Except for the root directory, it is in every

directory that the "`. .`" appears. And to the same inode as "`.`" that the "`. .`" always points.

2. `.` (single period) – which means the current directory

For us to list directories and files, we can use the `ls` command, including on Linux `..` and `.` directories.

```
ls -la
```

Directory

A sub-directory is contained inside another directory. A tree structure forms at the end of the directories and to see directory tree structure, use the tree command:

```
$ tree /etc | less
```

Typical of a file, a directory has an inode. As it connects each name with an inode number, it is a specially formatted file containing records. Under ex2/3 filesystem, it is quite vital to take note of the following limitation of directories:

- There is a chance for an unlimited number of subdirectories in Ext4 and other modern Linux filesystems

- In a single directory, there is a soft upper limit of about 10-15k files

- In a single directory, there is an upper limit of 32768 subdirectories

However, without any issues, using a hashed directory index, which is under-development, allows 100k-1M+ files in a single directory, according to the official documentation of ext2/3 filesystems. And related to directory, below are some bash shell alias commands:

```
alias ..='cd..'
alias d='ls -l | grep -E "^d"'
```

Linux directory management commands

For you to work with files and directories, here is a list of standard Linux commands:

Command	Description	Example(s)
diff command	Compares the content of any two files	`diff old.c new.c`
egrep command	Though, extended regular expression supported, it is the same as grep	`egrep -I 'err|cri|warn|' /var/log/messages`
grep command	In the specific files, it finds a specific search string	`grep "nameserver" /etc/resolv.conf`
more command	At a time, through text one screenful, it serves as a filter for paging.	`more /etc/hosts`
less command	The content of the specified file is seen by it.	`less resume.txt`
cat command	Displays the contents of a file	`cat data.txt`
file command	This detects the contents of the specified files.	`file /etc/resolv.conf`

find command	In a given directory, this searches for a file	`find $HOME -name "hello.c"`
locate command	Finding in which directory of a specified file is located	`locate file!`
chmod command	Changes the access permissions	`chmod 0444 dir1`
chgrp command	With the specified group name, this command transfers the group ownership of a given file to the group.	`chgrp dir1`
chown command	With the specified username, it transfers ownership of a file.	`chown username file`
ln command	From source to target, it creates an internal link	`ln -s /etc/hosts/tmp/link`
rm command	From the filesystem, this command removes the specified files, and unless the option -r is used, rm doesn't remove directories	`rm files!` `rm -r dir1`

70

cp command	Copies source to the target	`cp -r dir1 /path/to/dir2`
mv command	Deleting the source after copying to the target	`mv dir1 dir2`
cd command	cd changes to the home directory of the user without any parameters	`cd`
pwd command	This command displays the name of the working or current directory.	`pwd`
cd .. command	Go back to the previous directory.	`cd ..`
cd command	Change the current directory	`cd /etc/`
rmdir command	If it is already empty, this deletes the specified directory.	`rmdir dir1`
mkdir command	A new directory is created through this command.	`mkdir dir1`

Managing Directories

Since, from Nautilus, you can copy, move, delete, or create them, you must learn to treat your directories like files and related to files directories with the use of commands from a shell prompt.

Creating directories

For you to have a fresh sub-directory conceived, you must learn to write permission. It is at the /temp/ directory and the home directory, as well as the subdirectories that most users have these permissions. You will have to navigate to your new directory for you to use Nautilus in creating an original directory. In the window's blank potion, right-click and then choose to create a folder. Then, using the untitled folder with the highlighted text, a new folder icon will appear. Before you hit the 'enter' button, remember to give this new folder a name. When you attempt to use a shell prompt to have an original directory conceived, the `mkdir` command is all you need to use. You can replace the `<directory-name>` by simply type in: `mkdir <directory-name>` with the new directory's intended title.

Deleting directories

It is on the Desktop that you click and then **Trash** the icon or move it to the Trash after right-clicking on it to delete a directory from Nautilus. You will need to enter the `rmdir` command to delete a directory that is empty from the prompt of the shell. It is the `rm -rf <directory>` command that you will need for you to delete an unlikely empty directory and also all the things within such directory.

Dot directories

Dotfiles are also part of the applications created by "dot" directories. Also, other files required by the application, a hidden directory of configuration, is a directory for dot, and these files are a single hidden configuration file. Generally, these directories are user-specific non-configuration files, and their accessibility is to the user that has them installed.

Linux File Permissions

Since several users can have access simultaneously, and as a multi-user operating system, Linux is a clone of UNIX. Also, without any modifications, anyone can use Linux in servers and mainframes. However, because vital data can be removed, changed, or corrupted by malign or unsolicited individuals, this situation raises security concerns. As such, there are two levels of authorizations divided by Linux for adequate security, and they are:

1. Permission

2. Ownership

In Linux, a critical concept is ownership and permissions. We will begin the discussion with the Ownership as both of them will be examined.

Linux file ownership

There are 3 types of owners assigned for every directory and file on your Linux system.

Group:

There are multiple users contained in a user-group. Also, similar access permissions to the files will be given to all users belonging to a group. Several individuals will require access to a file if you have a project. You can go ahead and add all users to a group instead of manually assigning permissions to each user. Then, no one else can modify or read the files when you assign group permission to file.

User:

The owner of the file us a user, and you will be the owner if, by default, you are the one who creates a file. Thus, as an owner, you can also be called a user.

Other:

This case points to having access to a file by any other users. This type of user does not belong to a user group that owns the file or created the file. Mostly, this can be anyone else. Therefore, it is also referred to as setting permissions for the world when you set permission for others.

Ultimately, the question of distinction arises. How can you go about separating these three user types without exposing vital information from one group to another group? It is typical of hidden your image from your computer from your colleague who works on your Linux computer. Now, this is the case of permissions, and it is through user behavior that you can define it. For you to have a full grasp of the permission system on Linux, we may have to discuss more on it.

Permissions

For all the 3 owners discussed above, the 3 permissions below define every directory and file in your Linux system.

- **Execute**: as you can effectively run it, you have an extension ".exe" as an executable program in Windows. However, you won't be able to run an application unless the execute permission is set in Linux. And provided you set permission for write and read, though you can't run it, you might still be able to modify or see the program code.

- **Write**: you will have the influence of editing the contents of a file through the write permission. Also, in the directory, you can rename, remove, and add files as part of the authority you get from the write permission. You can assume where the file is stored, having no permission on the directory, and you have to write permission on file. The file contents can be modified by you. However, removing, moving, or renaming the file from the directory will not be possible for you.

74

- **Read**: you can read and open a file through the authority given to you by this permission. Also, you can list the content of a directory since you have the read permission.

SSH Command

Mainly, `ssh` command is included in every Linux system. The SSH client gets started through this command and on a remote machine, enables a secure connection to the SSH server. From a remote machine to logging, the `ssh` command is used for executing commands on the remote device and transferring files between the two computers.

SSH command in Linux

Over an insecure network and between two hosts, the provision of a secure encrypted connection is made by the `ssh` command. Also, for tunneling other applications, it can be used for file transfer and terminal access. From a remote location, you can securely run Graphical X11 applications over SSH.

Other SSH commands

With each of them having its page, besides the client `ssh`, there are other SSH commands.

- sshd – OpenSSH server
- sftp – file transfer with FTP-related command interface
- scp – file transfer with RCP-related command interface
- ssh-add – a tool to add a key to the agent
- ssh –agent – agent to hold private key for single sign-on
- ssh-copy-id – configures a public key as authorized on a server
- ssh-keygen – creates a key pair for public-key authentication

Chapter 9: Linux Terminals, Editors, and Shell

You can find help to get started with the terminal, whether it's been a while you have been using Linux or you are a new user of Linux. Without doubts, a terminal is a powerful tool with lots of values, and it is not something that can scare you. It is not really by reading a single book or article that you will be able to learn everything you need to know about the terminal. Firsthand, to play with the terminal takes experience.

Basic usage of terminal

You will see the bash shell on the application menu of your desktop when you launch a terminal. And by default, bash is what most Linux distributions use even though there are other shells. At the prompt, by typing its name, you can launch a program. Then, it is all a program from command-line utilities to graphical applications such as Firefox concerning everything you launch here. Though those functions are typical of programs, for essential file management, bash has a few built-in commands. And to launch it, you may not need to have the entire path typed to a program, unlike on Windows. For example, you will have to type the whole path to Firefox's .exe file when, on Windows, you attempt to open Firefox. You can type the command below on Linux:

```
firefox
```

To run it, after typing a command, go ahead and hit 'enter.' On Linux, programs don't have file extensions, and there's no need to add a .exe or anything else. Also, accepting arguments is part of terminal commands. You can utilize specific types of arguments concerning the program. For example, as arguments, web addresses are accepted by Firefox.

Installing software

Installing software from the terminal is one of the most efficient things to do. The fancy frontend of some terminal

76

commands that they use in the background, such as the Ubuntu Software Center, is the software management applications. Then, you can install them with a terminal background instead of doing it one after the other by selecting and clicking around applications. Also, you can have several apps installed with a distinct command. Since you can see the package management systems by other distributions, you can follow the following command when you intend to install a new software package on Ubuntu:

```
sudo apt-get install packagegename
```

Though it works similar to the Firefox command above, it may appear a bit complicated. With root (administrator) privileges, before launching `apt-get`, `sudo`, you can have the above line launched. Installing a package named `packagegename` is what `packagegename` will install by reading the argument apt-get program. However, it is as arguments that you can also specify multiple packages. For example, you could execute the command below to install Pidgin instant messenger and the Chromium web browser:

```
sudo apt-get install chromium-browser pidgin
```

Also, you could do it with a single command like the above if you want to install all your favorite software after installing Ubuntu. Since you can guess them reasonably quickly, the package names of your preferred programs are all you would need to know. Also, with the help of the tab completion trick, your guesses can be refined.

Text Editors for Linux Desktop

It makes it quite useful for some text editors to also double up as an IDE. Also, they are the default editors. In the Linux environment and for the Linux desktop environment in developing an application, these are quite helpful. The focus will be on a few text editors even though out there, there are a lot of text editors. As such, let's jump right into them:

GNU Emacs

For the Linux environment, one of the oldest text editors is GNU Emacs that has been here for quite some time. GNU's project founder, Richard Stallman, was the one who developed it. All around the world, for thousands of Linux programmers boast of it as their preferred and favorite text editors by using it. With the use of C and LISP, they were able to develop it. To install emacs on Linux Mint or Ubuntu, you can use the commands below:

```
linuxtechi@linuxtechi:~/Downloads$ sudo apt-get update

linuxtechi@linuxtechi:~/Downloads$ sudo apt-get install
emacs
```

There are some included unique features of GNU Emacs, which are:

- Extensive support and documentation

- Debugger interface extension

- News and mail options

For Linux Desktop, Atom and *notepadqq* can also be IDE and Text Editors, apart from these text editors.

Nano

In the UNIX operating system, another popular text editor used is Nano. In 2000, it was released, and it is the same as the Pico text editor. Also, to make it as an advanced and powerful text editor, it comes packed with some additional functionality. And it is in the interface only that it can run in a command-line. Here are a few unique features of Nano:

- Autoconf support

- Tab completion

- Auto Indentation

- Case sensitive search

Kwrite

It was in 2000 that Kwrite was first released to the public, and KDE developed this text editor. From KDE, along with the KParts technology, it is entirely based on the text editor for Kate. Making it a more powerful development environment, to a large extent, you can extend the Kwrite's functionality with the help of additional plugin installation. Also, along with encoding your file, it can be used to edit a remote file. On Linux Mint or Ubuntu, to install kwrite, use the command below:

```
linuxtechi@linuxtechi:~/Downloads$ sudo apt-get install
kwrite
```

A few unique features of Kwrite are:

- vi input mode
- Syntax highlighting
- Auto indentation
- Word completion

Eclipse

Eclipse editor can be a suitable option as an advanced and robust editor of code/text for frontend designers and developers. Since it contains several features that support developing and writing Java applications easily, it is entirely in JAVA that it was developed. Also, it is popular among Java developers. For anyone to accomplish extra language support, there may be a requirement for additional plugins if they need it. As the editor can have several advanced functionalities when you insert them with the help of additional plugins, the Eclipse IDE becomes even more powerful. And for the development of programs for COBOL, Ruby on Rails, C++, C, Python, and PHP, you can as well use it. For you to have eclipse installed on Linux Mint or Ubuntu, use the command below:

```
linuxtechi@linuxtechi:~$ sudo apt update

linuxtechi@linuxtechi:~$ sudo apt install eclipse
```

A few of Eclipse's unique features are:

- Plugin support
- For Java developer, tools for Java Development are included
- Open-source and free text editor

Kate

Loaded with the Kubuntu environment, as a default editor, you may have to know about the text editor of Kate if you are familiar with the Kubuntu desktop environment. Given that you can exploit it as a powerful IDE, you also have the opportunity of working with multiple files simultaneously since it is easy to use text editor, it is also a lightweight. Use the command below to install Kate on Linux Mint or Ubuntu:

```
linuxtechi@linuxtechi:~$ sudo apt-get install kate
```

Kate has some exceptional features, and they are:

- Sets indentation for documents automatically
- Auto-detects languages
- Supports several languages

- A powerful IDE

Gedit

Gedit comes loaded by default as a text editor in a GNOME desktop environment. Gedit follows similar objectives as it comes with a simple and clean user interface, and it is lightweight, just as the objective of GNOME to always offer functionalities that are straightforward and clean. With the GNOME desktop environment, getting access to it by the public didn't happen until 2000. It supports entirely for internationalized text as it is completely developed using C language. Gedit possess a few unique features, and they are:

- Supports several programming languages
- Supports internationalized text
- Syntax highlighting

Brackets

For the Linux environment, in 2014, the Brackets was launched by Adobe as a text editor. It has exciting packed features that make working with this editor a lot of fun as an open-sourced text editor. With a clean interface, it is also simple and easy to use. For programmers and web designers to get much-needed help, it is designed as a code editor and also as a text editor. They used JavaScript, CSS, and HTML to develop it completely. With its sophisticated qualities, a few quality text editors may not qualify for all the features it has even as it is on the lightweight side. For the installation on Linux Mint or Ubuntu, you can use the command below:

```
linuxtechi@linuxtechi:~$ sudo add-apt-repository
ppa:webupd8team/brackets

linuxtechi@linuxtechi:~$ sudo apt-get update

linuxtechi@linuxtechi:~$ sudo apt-get install brackets
```

Brackets text editor has a few unique features, which are:

- Focused visual tools Pre-processor support
- Inline editing
- Live preview

Sublime text editor

For the Linux environment, a text editor with so much esteem is a sublime text editor. You can use it as a development environment as well as a text editor; it is packed with several features. Along with various markup languages, it supports a lot of programming. Also, by extending its functionality to a great extent, the many available plugins have made the text editor more sophisticated. You can navigate to any file in your system or easily navigate to the code section through the help of the "Goto Anything" feature, and this is one of the distinctive highlights of this text editor. On Linux Mint or Ubuntu, to install the stable version of the sublime text editor, all you have to do is to refer to some specific commands. A few of the sublime text editor's exclusive elements are:

- Project-specific preferences
- Parallel editing of code
- Python-based plugin API
- Excellent command palette

Geany

For the Linux environment, one relatively recognized text editor that has the integration of the GTK+ toolkit is Geany. For developers and programmers, Geany can also work as an exceptional environment for development. Geany may be a suitable choice for you if you want a development environment and also a text editor. Other packages are not necessary to be installed with it for it to work quite well as it supports nearly all major programming languages and it is lightweight. For the installation of Geany on Linux Mint or Ubuntu, you only need to refer to a particular command. Geany has a few unique features, and they are:

- Interface that is easily pluggable
- Line numbering for easy tracking of code
- Lots of customized options
- Syntax highlighting for easy development
- Clean and easy to use interface

VIM

Vim will be your best choice if you prefer a lot of options and powerful performance to edit your text in an advanced text editor since the default "vi" editor in Linux may appear to bore you. As it is the default Linux text editor's advanced version, the meaning of vim is "vi improved," as suggested by the name. They have the specific need of the developers in mind when they are designing it. Also, for its highly configurable options, it is called a programmer editor. You can use it as a standalone GUI application or as a command-line utility, which is the same as the Vi editor. Here are a few unique features of VIM:

- Automatic commands
- Digraph input
- Split screen
- Session screen
- Tab expansion
- Tag system
- Syntax coloring

Introduction to Linux Shell

You are indirectly interacting with a shell if you are using any major operating system. And every time you use a terminal, you are interacting with a shell if you are running Linux Mint, Ubuntu, or any other Linux distribution. There are a few terminologies that are quite essential before we proceed, and we will discuss them in-depth in the following chapter.

Chapter 10: Basic Linux Shell Commands

On Linux, the command used for analysis is the shell. In a window of terminal emulation, the program users interact with is the shell. On Linux, the workstation's `mate-terminal` GUI is the emulation window. Also, it is an application like `PuTTY` or secure shell client; `SSH` secure on a system with Windows that, around the network, you can register into Linux. In some business or organizational settings, they make use of the Bourne Again Shell, `bash`. If you prefer, you can choose from some of the available shells like the TC-Shell, C-Shell, as well as the Bourne Shell. As specific features are appropriate to each of them, they all boast of the same characteristics. The features below belong to bash:

- As it remembers the last few commands, the history mechanism of the shell is indeed functional. In addition to a reference number, to list the previous few commands, you can make use of the `history` command.

For you to rerun a command, you can cut and paste from the history in a terminal emulation window of a workstation. Also, to rerun any command from history, the symbol `"i"` can be used.

- There is also "job control" for the shell, and in the background, you can run any programs that don't require any terminal interaction.

Available straightaway for other commands is the shell and the program `sort` in the background. In this case, the job control number "1" is printed by the shell as well as "3470," which is the process identity number. As it is running in the foreground, you can also use the special character Ctrl + z to suspend a program. You can then use `fg` to continue it in the foreground and even the `bg` command to put the program in

84

the background. You can refer to them by their job number if there is more than one running program in the background or suspended. As such, use the `jobs` command to list the status of all stopped or background jobs to see your jobs and their job numbers.

- You can write the scripts of shell commands, and similar to the compiled programs, you can invoke them as such by merely naming them. For example, we can first create a file in ~/bin containing the specific command to create a script that counts the number of C program files in this recent directory.

Before running it like normal, we can use the `chmod` command to make the file executable.

- With *if-then-else* statements, *for* loops, and *while* loops, bash is an interpretive programming language. When you type the command below, you will get more details about the Linux on-line documentation:

- The shell possesses numeric and string-valued variables.

The directory for home is `$HOME` as pre-set for some variables, and to see a list of assigned variables, type the `set` command.

- You can find it cumbersome to enter, or for the frequent execution of specific commands or groups of commands; you may want to assign `aliases`. For example, in a recent directory, to have the number of files of C program counted, we can assign an alias "countc" for the number counting of lines output using `wc` and have the files listed using `ls`.

- To *pipe* one program's output to another program's input, the shell boasts of such a facility. "`|`" is the symbol of the pipe. For example, in the `wc` program, we may have the output piped after we might have `cat` the file for us to count the number of words in file A.

- The *standard output* and *standard input* are the concept that most Linux programs and commands observe. An onslaught of output written by the program is the average output, and a flood of data read by the programs is the standard input. Most times, accompanying the terminal is most of these so that your screen can get this output while it is from your keyboard that you get the input. You can have the standard *redirected* to output and input through the shell.

- In your recent directory, to match filenames, the shell will expand the wildcards. For example, you can use a specific command to give a directory listing of the file with names `"anything.c"`

- Filenames are represented by the *argument* strings that the commands have. For example, in your home directory, the command can change the current directory to `"bin,"` and the meaning of *tilde* is that the shell is your home directory.

- For it to identify it, the process entails verifying to discover the built-in element is connected to the command and may then explore for a collection of directories by typing in a command name. The *search path* is what this means and included in the current directory is the search path, its subdirectory "bin," and your home directory. And through typing their names, you may invoke them after you must have written your programs. No matter what your current directory is, if

86

in the directory, you deposit such a program, it will be found and then run.

- By naming them, you can invoke commands. Most Linux commands are just programs that the shell executes. For example, the command `ls` can list the names of its files and read the recent directory as you get a specific result when you run it.

- There is an associated current directory that, similar to other programs, the shell has. When locating files, as the starting point, programs running on Linux use the current directory. In the filesystem of Linux, getting a different location by changing the recent directory is possible by using the `cd` command of the shell.

- The user can configure this command prompt. A dollar symbol preceded by "bash," as well as the version number of the bash program, is the default prompt.

With the use of the up-arrow keyboard, you can use previous commands of edit and recall with the help of an additional mechanism of bash. On top of the terminal, the final command will re-appear once you push the up-arrow, and to get the earlier commands, press the up-arrow once more. Hit on "RETURN" to have the command replayed. You can insert characters within the command or to delete by repositioning the cursor with the use of the key for back-arrow or from the end, remove characters by using the delete key to amend the command before rerunning it.

Shell Commands

Below, you will find a summary of the commands available. For each command, the reference on the manual page can give you more details. The command `man` can be used after your preferred name to see these online.

Database management
Available are Oracle and MySQL

Command	Description
MySQL-workbench	GUI interface for MySQL
Sqldeveloper	Oracle SQL Developer GUI interface
Mysql	Run the MySQL SQL interface
Sqlplus	Run the Oracle SQL interpreter

Word processing
LibreOffice is available and compatible with Microsoft Office.

Command	Description
LibreOffice	start applications for LibreOffice

Processing the text
For developing high-quality printed documents using Linux or other operating systems, an extensively used language of typesetting is `TeX`. When you intend to format manual pages, the standard typical Linux text formatting people generally use is another program collection built on `Troff`.

TeX

Command	Description
Dvips	Convert a DVI file to POST SCRIPT
Xdvi	DVI previewer
Pdflatex	latex formatter with PDF output
latex	latex formatter
tex	text formatting and typesetting

Troff

Command	Description
Pic	troff preprocessor for drawing pictures
groff	GNU troff interface for laserprinting
nroff	text formatting language
troff	text formatting and typesetting language
Grap	pic preprocessor for drawing graphs
tbl	prepare tables for nroff or troff
eqn	mathematical preprocessor for troff

General commands

Command	Description
aspell	interactive spelling checker
spell	check text for spelling error
acroread	PDF viewer
evince	GNOME PostScript previewer
fmt	simple text formatter

Programming

Available are these languages and programming tools.

FORTRAN

Command	Description
f95	GNU Fortran 95 compiler

JAVA

Command	Description
eclipse	Java integrated development environment on Linux
javac	JAVA compiler
appletviewer	JAVA applet viewer

C++

Command	Description

g++	GNU C++ Compiler

C

Command	Description
cxref	generate C program cross reference
indent	indent and format C program source
ctrace	C program debugger
gcc	GNU ANSI C Compiler
cb	C program beautifier

General

Command	Description
strip	remove symbol table and relocate bits
nm	print program's name list
Size	print program's size
make	maintain groups of programs

Other languages (not on all systems are these available)

Command	Description
asp	web page embedded language
mathematica	symbolic maths package

php	web page embedded language
squeak	Smalltalk
python	object-oriented programming language
perl	general purpose language
gcl	GNU Common Lisp
mattab	maths package
bc	interactive arithmetic language processor

Networking

Command	Description
google-chrome	web browser
firefox	web browser
curl	transfer data from a url
rsh	remote shell
rlogin	gaining access remotely to a Linux host
ssh	secure shell terminal or command connection
telnet	getting to another host by connecting through the terminal
wget	non-interactive network downloader
scp	copy of remote file for secure shell

rcp	remote file copy
sftp	program for transferring file in secure shell
tftp	trivial file transfer program
ftp	file transfer program

Messages between users

There is support for on-screen messages to other users and world-wide electronic mail in the Linux systems.

Command	Description
thunderbird	GUI mail handling tool on Linux
Mail	mail program for easy read or send
pine	vdu-based mail utility
wall	send a message to all local users

Printing

Expect the printer name to be given following a −p argument as most commands which can be used to print files. And as simple text files, files may be sent to the printers or for the laser printers; they may be processed in various ways.

Command	Description
a2ps-P*printer*	format text file in PostScript and print on laser printer

dvips-P*printer*	postprocess TeX file into PostScript and print on a laser printer
LPR-P*printer*	send a file to a printer

Direct from some applications or with the use of the GUI print manager; you can use the shell to print files. It is by name that you need to specify a printer, and some of them are:

Printer Name	Location
tl4_lw	Teaching Lab 4 (C/2.10) laser printer
tl2_lw	Teaching Lab 2 (C/2.05) laser printer
tl3_lw	Teaching Lab 3 (C/2.08) laser print
tl1_lw	Teaching Lab 1 (C/2.04) laser printer

Status

These commands alter or list information about the system.

Command	Description
printenv	display value of a shell variable
who	list logged in users
w	show what logged in users are doing
netstat	show network status

94

vmstat	report virtual memory statistics
lun	list user names or login ID
users	print names of logged-in users
last	show last logins of users
uptime	display system status
kill	send a signal to a process
Tty	print current terminal name
iostat	report I/O statistics
homequota	show quota and file usage
time	time a command
groups	show group memberships
stty	Set terminal options
script	keep script of terminal session
du	print amount of disk usage
reset	reset terminal mode
quota −v	display disk usage and limits
date	print the date
ps	print process status statistic

Information

Here are some shell commands that give information.

Command	Description

yelp	GNOME help viewer
info	displays command information pages online
man	displays manual pages online
apropos	locate commands by keyword lookup

Compressed files

To save space, you may need to compress files. You can use the following to examine and create compressed files.

Command	Description
zcmp, zdiff	compare compressed files
gunzip	uncompress gzipped files
zcat	cat a compressed file
uncompress	uncompress files
zmore	file perusal filter for crt viewing of compressed text
gzip	compress files

Manipulating data

You can use the command below to alter or compare the contents of files.

Command	Description
wc	count characters, lines, and words
look	find lines in sorted data

join	join files on some common field
uniq	report repeated lines in a file
gawk	pattern processing and scanning language
tr	translate characters
expand, unexpand	expand tabs to spaces and vice versa
split	split file into smaller files
diff	differential file comparator
sort	sort file data
cut	cut out selected fields of each line of a file
sed	stream text editor
comm	compare sorted data
paste	merge file data
cmp	compare the contents of two files
perl	data manipulation language
awk	Pattern processing and scanning language

File editors

You can amend and create files by using editors.

Command	Description
vi, vim	standard text editor

gedit	GNOME text editor
pluma	Mate GUI text editor
pico	easy text editor for vdus
ex, edit	line editor
xemacs	emacs with mouse action
emacs	GNU project Emacs

Files directory

You can handle files and create file directory through these commands.

Command	Description
lpq	spool queue examination program
touch	update modification and access times of a file
just	text justification program
tail	print last lines from file
head	give first few lines
rm, rmdir	remove (unlink) directories or files
grep	search file for regular expression
pwd	print working directory
find	Find files
mv	rename or move file type

file	determine file type
more, page	display file data at your terminal
cp	copy file data
mkdir	make a new directory
chmod	change file mode
ls	list and generate statistics for files
chgrp	change file group
lprm, cancel	Remove jobs from line printer queue
cd	change current directory
lpr	spool file for line printing

Logging out

Command	Description
logout	log out of a Linux terminal

You must take note that you must exit the Desktop Environment instead of a Linux workstation.

Chapter 11: Shell Scripting

For a Linux-based OS, a text file that has commands sequence is a shell script. The commands sequence of the shell script would have to be typed into a single script at a time into the keyboard. As an interpreter for commands set that you use to communicate with the system, the shell is the CLI, command-line interface's operating system. For them to save time, a user must repeatedly use the command sequence of a shell script. There are subcommands, comments, and parameters that the shell needs to follow, just like other programs. And it is by entering the file name on a command-line in the shell that users can initiate the sequence of commands. A shell script is known as a batch file in the DOS operating system as it also referred to as an EXEC in the mainframe VM operating system of IBM.

You can enter the command for the system execution since it is within the operating system of Linux that you will find the shell program. On a Linux computer, the shell program will start, providing the chance to have your commands entered through an interface when a terminal window is opened. The command-line interface is what this interface is referred to by people. On the screen, you can see the display of the output, and the shell executes it when a command is entered. Also, stored in a file, some commands can also be executed by the shell in addition to being able to execute and accept commands interactively. Shell scripting is recognized as the mode of this execution.

How shell script works

Giving the shell executive permission, making the script accessible to the shell, and writing the script are some of the fundamental steps involved with shell scripting. You can use a graphical user interface, GUI, word processor, or text editor to write shell script since it contains ASCII. The shell can interpret the language of a series of commands in the content of the script. Shortcuts, arrays, `if/then/else` statements, variables, and loops are some of the functions that shell scripts support. In a location that the shell can access, you can use the .sh or .txt extension to save the file once complete.

Background to the shell

In the 1970s, Ken Thomson developed V6 Shell, a shell program to start with Unix. Its scripting proficiency was quite lacking even as it was a shell with interactive features. In 1977, Bourne Shell came on board and for the root account; as the default shell, it remains in use today. And through the years, it has been quite useful through the scripting abilities. By the 80s, Korn Shell and C-Shell gave the public something to talk about as the highly popular shell variants. There was a drastic difference from the original shell as specific syntax has been brought by every one of these shells. As such, Bash is an extremely prominent shell today. As the unique Bourne Shell's massively enhanced variant, it stands for Bourne-Again- Shell.

Shell script applications examples

By typing one line at a time, you can save quite a lot of time from doing some repetitive task when you use a shell script. Below are some of the examples of applications that you can use a shell script for:

- Monitoring a system
- Executing routine backups
- Linking existing programs together
- Manipulating files
- Completing batch
- Creating a program or running a programming environment
- Automating the code compiling process

Shell script execution

As the shell's argument, all you have to do is to pass the script path if you want to execute a shell script. You need to pay attention to the fact that LF characters, Line-Feed, are required for terminating the lines by the shell. It is easy to run into errors if, on a Linux system, you attempt to execute shell script promptly or write it on Windows. For line termination, Carriage-return-Line-Feed, the combination of CR-LF is what Windows uses, and you will need to have it in LF-only conversion. For means to go about achieving this, you can check your Windows editor.

As a command, the shell script can be executed directly using another way. As your shell script's first line, you can insert the *hashbang* declaration below:

```
#!/bin/bash
```

Then, you can do some command to make your script file executable. Right now, without having to reference the shell explicitly, you can have the script file executed directly.

Benefits of shell scripts

Things are meant to be efficient and simple when you use shell script. It removes any interpretation issues since it is a similar syntax that it uses on the shell command-line that it uses in the script. Also, more than other programming languages, it requires less of learning curves and also faster when it comes to writing code for a shell script. However, if left unnoticed, this tends to prove extremely costly if there is an error in a shell script. Also, there may not be compatibility with different platforms connected with shell scripting, and more than individual commands; shell scripts can also be slower to execute. All the same, here are more advantages of shell scripts.

Portable:

When the shell itself is present, you can transfer a shell script to another Unix and Unix-related OS. Also, shell scripts are much more portable than C/C++ programs when you are in the process of transferring a shell script from different architectures like Sparc, MIPS, x86, and so on. You will have to attempt to run a C/C++, build the program, and copy the source code for you to transfer and use a C/C++ program. Then, if it uses the architecture-specific code, it may not work as expected.

Transparency:

Since it is a text file, you can check out the kind of actions the shell script is performing by viewing it quite easily. By contrast, it is if you have access to the source code or the source code wants to inform you that you can know the type of program in a language like C/C++. For example, it is possible to find out if any files are getting deleted by a shell script and then have those files copied to another place if you need those files. Also, because you may gain access to view the source code, shell scripts can be quite simple to diagnose than the regular programs. Though to avoid such errors, creating and checking programs are some of the responsibilities of a compliant shell script. You can as well create the directory as you look in the script code.

Easier to develop:

Inside a regular program written in C/C++, you can efficiently perform similar actions as the shell script. However, the shell script can be debugged and written far easier than a program like C/C++. By redirecting output, removing directories and files, and also execution of external commands, the shell is great for all these specific system administration tasks and more. For a much lower level operation, including manipulating data structures, invoking system calls, and so on, C/C++ programs tend to be much suitable for them.

Multiple commands combination:

One of the benefits of shell scripting is you can have multiple distinct sequences of commands as well as automating frequent tasks. For you to remember the direction in which you can execute multiple commands can be quite challenging than a single command. The Linux OS system sequence of boot-up is a perfect example here. For it to get the system into a proper state, the operating system executes a series of commands as one aspect of the boot-up process. The shell scripts that exist in the directory `/etc` are these commands. You may end up performing the process by hand in the absence of shell scripts, and a system booting process complexity will come to your realization if you take a look at these shell scripts types. The `/etc/profile` is an example of a shell script, and with the access of a user into the system, it can thus be executed.

Task automation:

Your executed tasks can be frequently automated when you use shell scripts, and this is the first benefit of it. Let's assume that daily, you need to perform a set of tasks. You can run these commands on the script after storing them in a file when you have to execute multiple commands on your Linux daily. For example:

- For too low or too high prices, when specific conditions are met, trigger an SMS or email as you parse the fetched data or fetch stock prices.
- As some log files appear to be growing every day, you can compress them.
- You can upload and archive a folder or file to a cloud storage facility every day like S3.

Features of Shell Scripting

Shell scripting is powerful

For every Linux-based operating system, you can get help almost for every one of them without any complaint, and it is convenient. You will have an excellent basis when you marge it with the standard accessible tool such as `sed`, `grep`, and `awk`.

Readability

It is much lower to develop anything that is unreadable with a shell script. You can certainly make use of some unique features of the shell that others do not know of them.

Regularly accessible

On all the programs you come across, you can always use shell scripting. By automating repetitive steps, it makes your life quite easier. All you need do is to insert your preferred commands in a file and run it happily after making it executable. As it is quick to master, so it is quite simple to learn.

Repeating

In your shell script, you don't need recurring similar statements every day. Create a compelling set of functions and consist of that in your existing and new shell scripts. While you can call your function "Display," resist it when you are about to use "echo."

Conclusion

To write workflow for epsilon, ETL, and several other tools to save time, quite useful for many organizations, is the scope of the shell scripts. And with the use of any of the shell scripts, professionals and users of Linux who want to automate tasks on Linux are the target audience of learning shell scripting technologies. For conditional programs that contain limited functions, loops, and statements, shell scripts can help to create these complex programs. Also, you can store data with shell scripts.

Chapter 12: Building Script

Using the language of programming for the shell are short programs, while the interpretation can be achieved through the shell scripts and a process of the shell. On Linux and other operating systems, they are quite ideal for task automation. For Unix-related OS, a program that provides the text-only, traditional interface is a shell program. You can read commands that you type into a terminal window as an all-text mode window, as well as console, which is an all-text display mode, and then run its primary function. The very common versatile and highly used *bash* is the default shell on Linux as groups of commands that you can translate, which is compiled or interpreted into a machine language form, and that can be wholly understood by the system's CPU, the central processing unit. You write computer programs with artificial, precise language, which is a programming language.

To create shell scripts, shell scripting language or shell programming language are the bash feature, and other Unix-related OS use shells with each of them containing the programming language with built-in features. You can easily have shell scripts created, and when you go online and in several books are available for a comprehensive selection of undertakings with or without notification. These factors are some of the advantages of using shell scripts. Also, in the Unix-related OS default installation, shell scripts are used extensively.

The first script

Here, you will see a useful introduction to shell scripts handling and creation with the following example. All previous lines of the screen of your monitor are cleared by the script, and on it, the text, *Good morning, world,* is written by it. You may not need a word processor but only need to have a text editor like *vi* or *gedit* opened when you want to create this script.

Also, with the functions of copy and paste used in the standard keyboard, you can copy the above code, open the text editor, and paste it into it. Then, the script is complete and quite close to running it after you have given a name to the file and have this plain text saved. By having the file name after a forward slash and a dot typed without any spaces between them and then hit on the 'enter' button, you will be ready to run scripts. For example, you can use the command below in the attempt to run it if you have the above script saved as *morning*:

```
./morning
```

Nevertheless, since you must first set the file to be *executable*, on the screen, you can see the message of error. In that situation, the script will not run. For the new files, *write* and *read* are the only permissions they have by default. With its option of *755*, you can make use of the chmod command to easily solve the problem. Using this, however in the same directory as the one below, you will have the ability not only to write and read the file, but you can also execute it:

```
chmod 755 morning
```

Then, while in the same directory and by typing the command below, you can prepare to run the script. To continue, hit the 'enter' button:

```
./morning
```

The operation process

The type of shell to use for the interpretation of the script and for locating the shell is the first three lines will tell the operating systems. As the directory /bin is its location, the shell is bash, and as such, the /bin/bash is what the line contains. For the operating system to receive its signal that it is offering the shell's location and name and other scripting languages, an exclamation mark, and a pound sign always precedes this instruction.

For you to dispense the command `clear`, it is the second line that the shell informs. With this easy command, you can remove all previous output and commands from the terminal or console window that there is a release of the command. On the screen, the *Good morning, world* phrase is what the shell gets from the third line. For whatever follows it to be repeated from the shell instruction, it uses the *echo* command. In a more advanced script, the quotation marks can make a big difference to use them as a useful programming drill even though they may not be necessary. An input data, an *argument* that the command `echo` receives is the *Good morning, world*, which is in slightly more technical terms. Also, scripts that people use freely are `echo` and `clear`, as is the case with other commands. For example, you will get the prompt to enter the next command, and you will have the entire previous output and commands removed when you type *clear* on the screen and hit the 'enter' button.

It isn't working!

There can be some reasons for the phrase *Good morning, world* not to appear at the top of the screen and some of them are:

1. For the *owner* of the file, they forget to change the permissions to *execute*.
2. In the same directory, the command was not issued where the file is located.
3. Instead of a text editor, a word processor was used to create it, and as such, the file is not a plain text file.
4. After the slash or period, space was inserted.
5. In the command, you omit or reverse the forward-slash or the period.
6. There is a difference in the name of the file and the one used in the command. For example, there can be a difference between capitalization, spelling, or even an extra or minor space.

7. You omit the word `echo`, and as a result, you made an error as you attempt to copy the code.

As the administrative user or the root, it is vital not to practice executing and writing scripts. You can damage the operating system with an improperly written script. Also, it could lead to necessarily reinstalling the operating system as a whole and result in the loss of valuable data in the worst-case scenario. You can easily use a command like `adduser` to quickly create one if an ordinary user account does not yet exist on the computer because of this reason.

Experiments

Before you make a move to more complicated examples, if you are a curious user, you can do a variety of instructive, simple experiments. With the suggestions below, they make up of code revision, using a different file name or a similar name of a file to save the changes, and then with the above explanation, executing them.

1. Attempt to have a few of the wording altered. For instance, have the line changed to *"Good morning, people!"* `echo`.

2. For the line that you will write on the screen, you can have a line, or more additional lines added as one horizontal space follow them at in any case, with each beginning having the word `echo`.

3. Concerning both lines of `echo`, you can also leave an empty line. Though by having `echo` typed on it, you can create a blank line, and that is all. It will be seen that this will not affect the result.

4. Then, have blank horizontal spaces inserted. Based on if you enter the primary reference marks before or after, there will be a different result.

5. To have a different location directory for the execution of the file. As such, when it is issued, you will have to add to the command name beginning, the executable script path. For example, if you have moved the file to `test`, a term of a subdirectory, you will have `./test/morning`.

6. You will want to add to the script file, some other command as another experiment like `df` that reveals the disk space usage, `uname`, which gives information about the hardware and software of a system, `pwd` that informs the present directory, and `ps` that explains the processes currently on the system. It is vital to understand that with any appropriate arguments or options, you can use these as well as other commands within the script.

Hello, World!

For you to have the shell script created:

1. *vi* is the text editor suitable for you to use for this, and within the file, have in its logic and commands of Linux that you required.

2. You will need to escape from vi, and before doing so, close after saving the file.

3. The executable form of the script is quite essential

4. Then, you can move on to the environment of production once the output satisfies you after testing the script.

5. A line in Bash, which is a straightforward program, informs a command of the computer. So, use your preferred text editor like vi to start it.

Necessary Commands of vi:

- To vacate vi:

```
Type :q after pressing ESC
```

- To search for a string:

```
type /wordToSearch after pressing ESC
```

- To jump to a line:

```
type :the line number after pressing ESC
```

- To quit after saving a file:

```
type :x after pressing ESC
```

OR

```
type :wq after pressing ESC
```

- To store a file:

```
type :w filename after pressing ESC
```

- To go into command mode:

```
press ESC
```

- To go into edit mode:

```
type I after pressing ESC
```

- To open a file:

```
vi filename
```

The script running after saving it

On the screen, a message of error is what the `./hello.sh` command displayed. Since for the `hello.sh` script, you have not set executed permission, it may end up not running the script.

Chmod command

To change the access permission of a file, you can make use of the `chmod` command. As follows, below is the syntax:

```
chmod ugo+rwx filename
```

Where:
- x: execute permission

- w: write permission

- r: read permission

- =: overwrite current permissions

- -: removes the permission

- +: adds the permission

- o: others

- g: groups

- u: users

Below is how you can express permission through a numerical way:

- 0: no permissions at all

- 7: read, write, and execute permissions

- 1: execute permission

- 2: write permission

- 4: read permission

Errors

The *robustness* of the program is often the measure used to differentiate a good and inadequate program. As such, when things go wrong, this is the ability of the program to handle these circumstances.

Exit status

When it finishes, returning to the exit condition is what every program that is well-written does. Zero will be the exit status when a program completes quite successfully. Then, in some way, the program failed if there is nothing more than zero for the exit status. For the program exit status in the scripts that you call, it is entirely vital to check them. Also, when they finish, there must be a meaningful return on the exit status of your scripts. Specific lines of code like $some_directory can be written for the creation system by the system administrator of a Unix.

If everything goes quite well enough, this way might not have been the wrong way of going about doing this. To the name that the $some_directory contained, the working directory was changed by the two lines and also in such a directory, delete the file. That is quite the projected action. And if the named directory in that $some_directory doesn't exist, what will then happen? Then, on the directory that is currently operational, the script will have the command rm executed and the command cd will fail. Indeed, not the planned action!

The exit category check

For you to respond and get the program's exit status, you can use several ways. First, the environment alternative of the $? and its contents require adequate observation and for the execution of the last command is an exit status that the $? will contain.

Except to revert zero's exit status and also one respectively, the false and true commands are programs that remain dormant. And for the previous program, the exit position is what is contained in the $? environment option. Hence, it is quite essential to have the exit category checked.

The cd command's exit level is examined in this variety, and on standard error, we can have the error message printed if it's not zero and with 1 as the exit status, have the script terminated. However, we can save ourselves a few typing efforts by using some smarter techniques even when this happens to be an effective way-out to the crisis. Since it is the given commands of the exit status that it evaluates, we can make use of the statement if precisely as the next approach to attempt.

If there's a success with the command cd, we can check it here. And for the indication that an error has happened, a code of 1 is the program exit. As for the output is the error message, you can then execute rm.

Chapter 13: Basic Bash Shell Commands

In a circumstance that a directory tends to be a *root directory* by possessing no parent directory or within a single other directories, it is a *subdirectory* that is known as "parent." Thus, modern filesystems have folder or directory trees. And you can always get to the root directory by going from child directory to parent directory, which is typical of traversing backward through the file tree. Though Unix and Unix-like system only have \., a single root directory, such as Windows' drives: *A:* \, *C:* \, etc., some filesystems have multiple root directories.

`pwd / ls / cd`

As we refer to the *working directory* or the current directory, it is always within some directories that the user is always using when working within a filesystem. With `pwd`, print the working directory of the user. Using `ls`, make a list of files and child directories, etc., that is, the content of this directory. Here, you need to pay attention to some of these points:

- Instead of `ls  -1  -a`, you can sometimes chain flag like `ls  -la`
- Have a combination of several flags such as `ls  -1-a`
- Reveal file details with `ls  -1`
- Using `ls  -a` to reveal hidden ("dot") files

Using cd (change directory) to change to a different directory and the parent directory, the shorthand for `cd` is `cd`. To home directory normally /home/username or similar directory, the shorthand for `cd` ~ or simply cd is `cd`. For this directory, *cd.* may not make any much impact since . is shorthand. Use *cd* – to go back to the most recent directory. And by using *cd*

`../,,,etc.`, you can jump multiple directories levels. To home directory user, `cd ~user` means `cd`.

`;` / `&&` / `&`

Commands are the things that you type into the command-line and stored somewhere on your computer; they always execute some machine code. Sometimes, a built-in Linux command is this machine code, and sometimes also, it is some code that you wrote yourself and perhaps an app. Occasionally, right after another, we will want to run one command, and we can as well use the ";" (semicolon) to do that:

The meaning of the semicolon is `l` first *(ls)* lists the contents of the working directory, and then `l` *(pwd)* prints its location. Then, `&&` can be used to chain commands, which is another useful tool. If the command to the left fails, the command to the right will not run. On the same line, you can use both `&&` and `;` multiple times.

Even if the first one fails, the second will run with `;`. There is a completely different function fulfilled by & even when it looks similar to &&. Usually, before it gives you access to enter another one, the command-line will wait for that command to finish when you execute a long-running command. You will be able to perform a new command while an older one is still going and also prevents this from happening when you put & after a command.

It is essential to know that we assume that the process or job is *"backgrounded"* when, to hide it, we make use of `&` after a command. Then, use the `job` command to see what background jobs are currently running.

Getting Help

man

For you to bring manual for that command (with *q*, quit `man`), type man before nearly any command.

`-h`

And for you to bring up a help menu for that command, type `--help` or `-h`.

Viewing and editing files

nano / nedit

For people or beginners that want to learn a million shortcuts, as a command-line text editor with minimalistic characteristics, `nano` is a great editor. For the first few years of coding career, it will be sufficient for any developer or programmer. As it allows for syntax highlighting, drag-and-drop, point-and-click editing, `nedit` opens up an X Window as a small graphical editor. When you plan to make some changes to a script and then rerun it over, you may want to use `nedit` for that. Atom, Notepad++, gedit, vim, vi, emacs, and some others are other common editors like graphical user interface, GUI or command-line interface, CLI. Others are VS Code, Light Table, and Micro. The syntax highlighting, search and replace, and some other things are the basic convenience that all modern editors provide. Though `nano` and `nedit` don't have as many more features as emacs and vi(m), their learning curves tend to be much steeper. You will discover the one that works for you after trying out a few different editors.

head / tail / cat / less

File's few first lines are the `head` outputs. Though the default is 10, the number of lines to show is specified by the `-n` flag. File's last few lines are the `tail` outputs. Beginning from the *N* -th line with `tail -n +N`, you can get the end of the file or, like above, you can get the last *n* lines. Usually, the terminal, but what sends files to the standard output stream and

117

concatenates a list of files is `cat`. You can use it to view files quickly, and with multiple files or just a single file, you can make use of the `cat`. But, here, pay close attention; you may be accused of a UUOC, Useless Use of Cat if you use `cat` in this way. You may not worry yourself too much about that because it's not a big deal.

For you to quickly view a file, another tool is `less` as it opens vim –like, read-only window. `more` is another command. However, `less` has a higher recommendation than `more` since it provides a superset of the functionality of `more`. At their `man` pages, you can learn about `more` and `less`.

Creating and deleting directories and files

mkdir / rm / rmdir

For you to create new, empty directories, you can use *mkdir*. As this is non-recoverable, you need to be cautious as using `rm` can remove any file. Then, with the *–i* flag, an *"are you sure?"* prompt can be removed. With the use of `rmdir`, you can remove an empty directory. Then, you could see a reference to its parent directory (..) as well as a reference to the directory itself (.) when you `ls` *–a* in an empty directory. It is only empty directories that `rmdir` removes.

However, using `rm` *–rf* (*–r* = recursive, *–f* =force) cannot remove a directory and all of its content.

touch

It is to modify file timestamps that `touch` was created. However, you can also create an empty file using it and such as `nano`, by opening it with a text editor, you can create a new file. You can also edit the file. Also, `touch` can be used as well. Note: ^z (Ctrl+z) is the background a process. Then, hit ^z with editing file. Shown by the jobs command where `N` is the job index, use `kill` `%N` to kill a background process. While it

118

is running, press ^c (Ctrl+c) to kill the current (foreground) from processing.

History of command, links making, and copying and making files

mv / cp / ln

To rename or move a file, use mv. You can mv a file to a new file, to rename it, or keep the same file or mv a file to a new directory. Then, copy a file using cp. And for you to create a hard link to a file, use ln. Also, you can get a soft link created to a file with ln -s. In memory that contains a file, the same actual bytes are referenced in hard links, and while it points to those bytes, the soft links refer to the original fine name.

Command history

For you to be able to rerun and complete commands, there are two main features that you can get from bash. *Tab completion* is the first feature. For guessing the precise action you are attempting to take, you only need to press the key <tab> after you have the first section of the command typed. Then, you will complete the command after you must have typed *ls t* and press the TAB key. Note that if an ambiguity case arises, it may be required of you to press the <tab> several times. And as for your previously typed commands, you can get the short history of them since bash keeps them, and by typing ^r(Ctrl+r), you will have the chance to have a search through for those commands. If you want to see the command history search, hit ^r(Ctrl+r).

Processes, disk usage, and directory trees

ps / du / df

For the hard drives of your system or the disks, if you want to know the amount of space your files have taken up, df will be there to show you. If you go through this command, you will notice that the meaning of -h is "human-readable" and not "help." And rather than writing out integer, huge bytes number, to display disk or file sizes, it is G for gigabytes and K for kilobytes that some commands use. For the subdirectories of a specific directory, the file space usage is what the du shows. You may use df for you to discover the free space of a particular hard drive. Also, using du will allow you to know the quantity of a directory's space. From the specified directory, the flag --max-depth=N are directories N levels fewer or down, which du takes. For current processes running by the users, it is shown by the ps.

tree/ mkdir -p

It is only a single directory, by default, that mkdir makes. As such, using mkdir only, it may be hard for you to make d/e/f since d/e directory has no existence. And also, if there is no such existence for them, all directories in the path can be made when we pass to mkdir from the -p. Also, when we have a nicely-formatted directory printed, we can visualize the structure of a directory better through the help of the tree. With a specified directory, in the beginning, the whole structure of the tree is printed by it. However, using the flag -L, you will have the power of restricting it to a particular number of levels. Then, using -prune, in the output of the tree, the empty directory can be hidden. You must know that the directory that is not that empty or the "recursive empty" will also be removed by this command, but which has in them other recursively empty directories or other empty directories.

Miscellaneous

exit / logout / passwd

You can use passwd to have the password of your account changed. To verify it, you may have to provide the current password you are using. Then, to forestall any typo situation, it will want you to enter your new password two times. In a situation where it is only a user account that you have, the shell you have logged in will exit with the use of logout. And to have any shell exited, then use the exit.

*clear / ***

For you to have your new terminal line moved on to the screen top, then run `clear`. Below the line of your current prompt, you will have blank lines added to them by this command. Thus, you can clear your workspace with this. And in the situation of looking for specific files, wildcard, also known as Kleene Star, *, is perfect for it. And since it is equivalent to more characters or zero, in a command, you can make use of the glob several times.

Processor usage, memory, and disk

htop / top

The processes that are running recently as well as their memory usage, owners, and many can be displayed through the `top`. The variant of the `top`, which is interactive and enhanced, is an `htop`. You need to know that the display processes can be restricted by using a `username` only to those owners while passing the flag `-u username`.

ncdu

Typical of an enhanced `du`, it is the file space usage overview, which is navigable that the `ncdu` offers. Also, it is a `vim`-related window with a read-only feature that it can open. When you want to quite, press `q`.

REPLs

Though they utilize it for specific programming languages, typical of the command-line is Real-Evaluate-Print Loop, which is REPL. While you can use the function `quit()` for you to quit, the command `python` is what you can use to open the Python REPL. Also, using the command `R`, you can have the R REPL opened as well as using the function `q()` for you to quit. With the command `scala`, you can also have the Scala REPL opened and the command `:quit` when you want to quit. With Java REPL, you can use command `jshell` to have it opened and `/exit` command for you to quit. Optionally, with the use of ^d(Ctrl+d), you can exit any of the REPLs. As ^d signifies the input's end on Unix, it is also the marker for the end of the file, EOF.

-v / --version / -version

For most programs and commands to have the software version, they possess the flag --version or -version. This information tends to be available easily for most applications, even though there is a less intuitive factor for most. You need to take notice of the use of -v by some programs for the version flag, and this means 'verbose' for using -v by others, which, while debugging information or printing several diagnostics, can run the application.

Environment variables

Within your bash shell, the tenacious variables that you can use and create are the environment variable, and "env vars" is their short-term. You can use it with the sign of a dollar ($), and for their definition, they make use of the equal sign (=). When you use printenv, the entire recently-defined env vars can be seen. Using the sign =, you can have a new environment variable set. You must be careful to note that your = has no space after or before. Using echo with a preceding sign of $, you can have a particular env var printed to the terminal. Attempt to surround other whitespace or all spaces around the environment variables with the quotes ("..."). Also, be cautious because you won't get any warning and will probably overwrite an env var by having a value reassigned to it. Apart from those above, you can also use the command export to define the env vars. Also, they can be available to sub-processes, which are commands you called from this shell when you provide the meaning this way. When you use the command unset or leave the right-hand side of the = blank, you can have the environment variables unset.

Chapter 14: Advanced Bash Shell Commands

As a fairly powerful programming language and not only appropriating seam connecting the user and the kernel of the operating system, the shell is a command interpreter. And by *gluing* together compiled binaries, utilities, tools, and system calls, you can build applications through a straightforward device called a script inside a shell program. By a shell script, available for invocation are indeed the whole catalog of Unix tools, utilities, and commands. Also, there can be additional flexibility and power to scripts through external shell commands like loop and testing constructs, if that were not enough. Without requiring a complete compactly designed programming language with plenty of the bells and whistles, it is to administrative systems tasks as well as other routines, repetitive jobs that shell scripts exceptionally lend themselves.

Introduction to Regular Expression

A sequence of characters is an expression. Metacharacters are those characters that have an interpretation beyond and above the factual connotation that they have. For example, a speech by someone may be denoted by a quote symbol and ditto the subsequent symbols for a meta-meaning. Metacharacters or characters that specify or match patterns are regular expressions. Here are some of the components that a regular expression contains:

- **Modifiers**. By modifying, for the range of text that the regular expression is to match, these narrow or expand it. The backlash, brackets, and asterisk are some of the modifiers.
- **An anchor**. For the match between the text line and the regular expression, it is the anchor that designates this position. For example, anchors are $ and ^.

- **A character set**. These characters retain their literal meaning. And with no metacharacters, a character set is the simplest type of regular expression.

String manipulation and text search are the significant applications aimed at regular expression, and it is a part of a sequence or a string that matches a set of characters or a single character for a regular expression.

- Escaped "angle brackets"–– \<...\> –– mark word boundaries.

Since otherwise, they possess only their literal character and meaning, the angle brackets need to be escaped.

The word "the" matches "\<the\>" and not the words "*others*," "*there*," "*them*," etc. The only way to be sure that a particular regular expression works is to test it.

- The backlash –– \ –– their character gets interpreted as it escapes a unique character.

Instead of its regular expression meaning of end-of-line, a "\$\" reverts to its literal meaning of "$." Also, the literal meaning of "\' is a "\\."

- Brackets – [...] – for a single regular expression to have a match, enclose a set of characters.

There is a match for common word patterns with the combination of sequences of bracketed characters. "there is a match between *yes, Yes, YES, yEs*, etc., and "[Yy][Ee][Ss]." Another matches for any Social Security number are "[0-9][0-9][0-9][0-9][0-9][0-9][0-9][0-9][0-9].

Except for those in the range b to d, all characters match "[^b-d]." Inverting or negating ^ is a typical instance for the meaning of the following regular expression (in a different context, taking on a role similar to !).

Any digit or lowercase letter that matches "[a-z0-9]".

In the ranges of *k* to *y* and *b* to *P*, any of the characters that match "[B-Pk=y]."

In the range of *c* to *n*, any of the characters that match "[c-n]."

The characters x, y, or z match "[xyz]."

- The end of a regular expression matches the end of a line, which is the dollar sign -- $ --.

Matching blank lines is "^$."

At the end of the line, XXX matches "XXX$."

- The beginning of a line matches the caret --^-- and which negates the meaning of a set of characters in a regular expression depending on context sometimes.
- Except for a newline, any one character matches the dot --.—

Though, not *13* additional character missing, "13" matches *13 + at least one of any character, including space: 1133, 11333.*

- As well as *zero* instances, any number that has the repetition of the regular expression or character string matches the asterisk --*--.

"1133*" matches *11 + one or more 3's: 113, 1133, 1133333,* and so on.

- Extended regular expressions. Additional characters that the basic set have also. It is in *Perl, awk,* and *egrep* that they use it.
- One or more of a preceding regular expression matches the plus --+--. Though it does not match zero occurrences, it is the same role as in the * that it serves.
- Zero or one of the previous regular expression matches the question mark --?--. It is for matching single characters generally.
- Escaped "curly brackets" --\{\} – the previous regular expression to match is the indication of the number of the occurrences.

Because it is the literal character meaning that they only have otherwise, it is quite vital to escape the curly brackets. Technically, the fundamental regular expression arrangement does not correlate with this usage.

For the character in the 0 to 9 range, "[0-9]\{5\}" matches precisely five digits.

Note: as the non-POSIX compliant, classic `awk` version with a regular expression, curly brackets are not available. However, without being escaped, they have permission from the option `-re-interval` which gawk has. The versions that have no obligation from escaping the curly brackets are some **egrep** and **perl**.

- Parentheses – () – has in its enclosure a set of regular expressions. Using expr in substring extraction, with the following operator " | " they tend to be quite useful.
- The regular expression or the --|-- the alternate character set matches it.

As do the GNU utilities, there is support for some version of *ex*, *ed*, and *sed* the lengthy regular expressions escaped version in the above description.

- Character Classes of POSIX. [:class:]

For the match of identifying characters range, this is an alternate method.

- [:xdigit:] matches hexadecimal digits. This is the same as 0-9A-Fa-f.
- [:upper:] matches uppercase characters of alphabets. As such, A-Z tends to be the same.
- [:space:] matches whitespace characters (horizontal and space tab).
- [:print:] (printable characters) in the scope of ASCII 32 – 126, it matches characters. Though adding the space character, this tends to be similar to the [:graph:] below.
- [:lower:] characters of the alphabet with a lowercase that matches. The a-z is quite the same as this.
- [:graph:] (graphic printable characters). Though excluding the space character, in the scale of ASCII 33 – 126, it matches characters. This is similar to [:print:] above.
- [:digit:] matches (decimal) digits. This is equivalent to 0-9.
- [:cntrl:] matches control characters.
- [:blank:] matches a tab or space.
- [:alpha:] matches alphabetic characters. This is equivalent to A-Za-z.
- [:alnum:] matches numeric or alphabetic characters. This is equivalent to A-Za-z0-9.

Conclusion

Thank you for making it through to the end of *LINUX Command-Line for Beginners: A Comprehensive Step-By-Step Starting Guide to Learn Linux from Scratch to Bash Scripting and Shell Programming*, let's hope it was informative and able to provide you with all of the tools you need to achieve your goals whatever they may be.

Chances are if you've made it to this point, it is because you want to know how you can navigate through the Linux operating system as well as having a clear grasp of the several command-lines and also the best ways of using them. You have made it to this point because you want to know all about many different pieces than Linux operating system comprises and also how you can install different distributions of Linux.

You will see that you can deal with types of installations for servers and also their roles. Reading through this book, you have learned how you can use Linux as a virtual machine inside another operating system, what dual booting is all about, and how you can boot Linux with the use of live CD/DVD.

In this book, you have read about Linux kernel and the operating systems, Linux directory structures, some of the fundamental Linux shell commands, how you can work with the disk, media, and data, and so much more. For you to get an understanding of how you can ideally use Linux and some of the associating programs, this book has shed enough light on essential terminals, editors, and shell.

CPSIA information can be obtained
at www.ICGtesting.com
Printed in the USA
BVHW050849120421
604725BV00004B/187